A Disciple's Path

Deepening Your Relationship with Christ and the Church

Leader Guide

James A. Harnish with Justin LaRosa
and Barbara Dick

Abingdon Press
Nashville

A DISCIPLE'S PATH LEADER GUIDE

Copyright © 2012 by Abingdon Press

This book is printed on acid-free paper.

ISBN 978-1-4267-43481

13 14 15 16 17 18 19 20 21—10 9 8 7 6 5 4

MANUFACTURED IN THE UNITED STATES OF AMERICA

CONTENTS

How to Use This Leader Guide

A Disciple's Path combines a uniquely Wesleyan understanding of growth in God's love and grace (Week 1) with the time-tested practices of spiritual discipline expressed in the vows of membership when we promise to participate in the ministries of the church by our prayers, presence, gifts, service, and witness. (Weeks 2-6). The program enables participants to practice those disciplines in Christian community with other disciples who are walking the same path through a six-week group experience.

A Disciple's Path provides the following components for your journey together:

- **Daily Workbook:** Five daily readings with reflection questions for each week of study; this material is to be completed by participants prior to each weekly group session.

- **Companion Reader:** Biblical and theological insights on each week's theme from a distinctively Wesleyan perspective.

- **CD-ROM:** Handouts, including customizable templates that may be adapted to fit the unique mission, vision, ministry, and organization of any congregation; two PowerPoint presentations; and sample e-mails.

- **Leader Guide:** Leader helps and session plans for each week of study.

- **Ancillary Products:** Bookmark, window cling, key tag, and wristband with key words and ideas to promote awareness and serve as daily visual reinforcements for participants (optional).

Using these components, you will lead your participants over the course of six sessions—with the option of an introductory session or pastor's coffee on what it means to be a United Methodist. The introductory session is optional but recommended, particularly for new member classes and groups wanting a refresher course in basic United Methodist beliefs and practices. The *Daily Workbook* engages participants in five days of reflection on scripture and teaching material while guiding them in practicing the discipline(s) for that week. These daily reflections become the basis of discussion, sharing, and accountability in the weekly small-group experience. Participants are encouraged to read the corresponding chapter in the *Companion Reader* before the group session to enrich and deepen their understanding of each week's topic.

The first session begins with an overview of *A Disciple's Path* and provides a framework for spiritual growth in the Wesleyan tradition. Group members will be at different places on the spiritual journey, and all of them will have the opportunity to respond to Jesus' invitation to follow him on the road of discipleship and to engage in the spiritual practices embedded in the membership vows of The United Methodist Church. The remaining sessions outline practices related to the membership vows:

Prayer: *Prayer and Scripture Reflection*—Spending time each day in prayer and in studying and reflecting on the Bible to experience the living word of hope in the written Word.

Presence: *Corporate Worship and Small-group Community*—Celebrating God's presence in worship with a faith community; experiencing Christian community in a small group to pray, learn, and grow together.

Gifts: *Financial Generosity*—Practicing Christian stewardship through the biblical discipline of tithing.

Service: *Gifts-based Service*—Discovering our spiritual gifts and participating in God's work through the ministry of the church and in our daily lives.

Witness: *Invitational Evangelism*—Sharing the joy of our journey and inviting others to experience God's love and become disciples of Jesus Christ.

A Disciple's Path can be used for new member orientation classes, in ongoing classes and small groups, or as a congregation-wide emphasis. However you use the study, be sure to have copies of the *Daily Workbook* and the *Companion Reader* available for participants prior to Session 1. If you are having an introductory session or pastor's coffee, distribute the books at that time or make them available for participants to pick up at a designated place and time prior to Session 1.

An Overview

As group leader, your role will be to facilitate the group sessions. All groups are different in composition. Some group members have followed Christ since they were children, while others may be brand new followers who have had very little experience with Christ or the church. Most of the group members will have made a profession of faith, but be aware that some may be exploring and may not have made this commitment. No matter where your group members begin, we believe that every follower of Jesus is involved in an ongoing process of transformation. *Note: Ideal group size is 8-15 participants.*

Below is an outline of two format options for structuring your group time. You may wish to follow one of the proposed formats, or you may choose to adapt them to meet your unique needs. The times listed are estimates and can be altered according to the flow and pace of your group.

60 Minute Option

Sign in / Objectives	2 minutes
Opening Prayer	1 minutes
Biblical Foundation	2 minutes
Daily Workbook Discussion	45 minutes
Looking Ahead to Next Week	5 minutes
Take Home Message / Closing Prayer	5 minutes

90 Minute Option

Sign in / Objectives	2 minutes
Opening Prayer	1 minutes
Biblical Foundation	2 minutes
Daily Workbook Discussion	55 minutes
Optional Activity	20 minutes
Looking Ahead to Next Week	5 minutes
Take-home Message / Closing Prayer	5 minutes

The more prepared you are as the leader, the better the experience will be for the group. Familiarizing yourself with the various elements of the session format or plan will help you to design the flow for your group sessions.

Sign In/Objectives

Each week have group members sign in and pick up a name tag. The first time you have folks sign in, ask for their names, e-mail addresses, and phone numbers so that you can create and print a customized group roster (sign-in forms for the pastor's coffee and group sessions are provided on the CD-ROM). The following weeks they may simply put a checkmark beside their names on the roster to sign in. Even if you have participants sign up online or pre-register for the group in some other way, signing in each week will help you to keep track of attendance so that you may follow up with those who have missed.

Then, begin the session by providing a verbal outline of the objectives for the session (you also might choose to write these on a board or chart). These are included in your leader guide materials each week.

Opening Prayer

The opening prayer can be done in a variety of different ways. You can read the prayer provided in the session outline, choose a prayer from the week's readings in the *Daily Workbook*, bring a printed prayer for the group to read in unison, offer a spontaneous prayer, or have a group participant offer a prayer. (After the first session, you may choose to recruit group members to offer the opening and closing prayers.)

Biblical Foundation

This is the foundational Scripture passage for the session. Invite a group member to read it aloud each week. You might consider having one person read it from one translation and another read from a different translation.

Daily Workbook Discussion

Whether you follow the 60-minute or 90-minute plan, engaging group members in reviewing and discussing the readings in the *Daily Workbook* is critical to the effectiveness of the group session. Alerting participants that you will be reviewing the readings in each session increases the likelihood that they will complete them.

The *Daily Workbook* Discussion is designed to help the group dig deeper into the spiritual practice for the week. Because people learn in different ways, we encourage you to employ different methods week to week for engaging the group. For example, one week you might choose to stick with lecture and discussion, while the next you might invite a guest speaker or lay witness or incorporate a video clip (not included) or some other media that pertains to the topic. If the group is larger than fifteen people, you may want to break into

small groups for the discussion and activity. If several people in the group have little experience with spiritual practices, it may be beneficial to have more instructional time.

Optional Activity

If you follow the 90-minute format, this section outlines an additional activity for the group. It includes having the group engage in methods of Scripture reflection and prayer that they have already studied during the week, offering opportunity for deeper familiarity and comfort with the method.

Looking Ahead to Next Week

Each session allows time for discussing the upcoming week's topic. Talk briefly about the topic, identify the pages in the *Daily Workbook* and *Companion Reader* that participants need to read and complete before the next session, and cover any special preparation required for the coming week.

Take-home Message / Closing Prayer

At the conclusion of the session, have each participant share his or her "Take-home Message"—the key message that he or she will take home from the group session. Don't be afraid of silence. If no one shares after 10 seconds, ask, "Would anyone be willing to share first?" If no one responds after an additional 5-10 seconds, provide an answer. Then ask for other comments. You might choose to facilitate the take-home message while the group is standing in a circle holding hands prior to the closing prayer.

At the first session, read the prayer provided, offer a spontaneous prayer, or select a prayer from the *Daily Workbook*. After the first session, you may choose to recruit a group member to offer both the opening and closing prayers.

Helpful Hints for Preparation as a Facilitator

- **Check out your classroom.** Before your group is scheduled to meet, make sure the meeting environment is ready. Have enough chairs? Lighting adequate? Have all the supplies you need?

- **Choose the format.** Decide on the session format (60 or 90 minutes) and the various elements you will use for each group session. Be sure to communicate dates and times to participants in advance.

- **Offer Welcome.** If you have the group members' names and phone numbers, call and welcome them prior to the initial session.

- **Set the tone.** As the leader, you will set the tone for the group. Set expectations during the first session and cover the ground rules for interaction.

- **Pray for your group.** All group members are people arriving at different stages from different experiences with different insights, none of which is the facilitators' job to evaluate. Pray for God to work in the lives of everyone in your group.

- **Read and complete all reading and activities.** Make note of the insights and questions you feel are most important from the *Daily Workbook* and *Companion Reader.*

Helpful Hints for Leading the Class

- **Keep first things first.** Your primary role is to help the class members move toward discovery, insight, and understanding—as individuals and as a group.

- **Welcome everyone.** Make an effort to personally welcome and greet each person as she or he arrives.

- **Silence cell phones.** Plan to keep interruptions to a minimum. At the start of each session, ask people to turn off or silence cell phones.

- **Always start on time.** Honor the time of those who are on time. If you don't do this faithfully from the first meeting, people will arrive later and later each time.

- **Encourage others to lead in prayer.** Remember, for many people it takes time before they feel comfortable praying out loud.

- **Don't put people on the spot.** Some people are very comfortable sharing; others are not. Ask people to offer answers, testimonies, and stories as they are comfortable.

- **End on time.** Regardless of where you are in the lesson, when the clock rolls around to the "decided" ending time, call time and give group members the opportunity to leave if they need to. Then wrap up as quickly as you can. This communicates that you value and respect people's time.

- **Address after-session conversations.** Be prepared for people who want to hang out and talk at the end. If you need people to leave by a certain time, make this clear during the meeting. Be aware of nursery closing times.

- **Thank people for coming.** Let them know you're looking forward to seeing them next time.

Helpful Hints for Facilitating Group Discussion

- **Share your enthusiasm.** Communicate the value of participating in group discussions, completing exercises, and reading the relevant material in the *Daily Workbook* and the *Companion Reader*.

- **Limit your talk.** The ratio of facilitator talk time to participant talk time is ideally 20/80. If you talk most of the time, the group may learn to listen rather than to engage. Your task is to draw conversation from the group members.

- **Give everyone a voice.** Don't hesitate to break into smaller groups to discuss some of the questions. This encourages greater participation by everyone— especially those uncomfortable in a large group setting. We want everyone to have a voice.

- **Encourage "safe" participation.** While you want everyone to participate, be careful not to put anyone on the spot. Let the group members know upfront that they don't have to answer questions they are uncomfortable answering. It is always okay to say no or to pass. Give people freedom to participate as they feel comfortable.

- **Be neutral.** Try not to interrupt, judge, or minimize comments/input. And don't begin with preconceived expectations.

- **You are not expected to be the expert.** None of us has all the answers. . . . Seek together. A facilitator is not a lecturer, sage, answer giver, or expert. Allow the Holy Spirit to be "in charge." Remember, it's God's plan. When group members look to you for definitive answers, focus feedback on sharing ideas rather than on giving advice. If issues or questions arise that you don't feel equipped to deal with or answer, consult with the pastor or a staff member at your church or refer a class member to them for research to bring back and share with the class.

- **Silence is okay.** It's okay to wait for someone to answer. You don't need to answer something yourself if no one speaks up right away. Avoid filling silence too quickly. After a moment, ask, "Would anyone be willing to share?" If no one responds after a time, try rephrasing the question and ask it again.

- **Use open-ended questions.** Ask, "What do you think about _____?" rather than "Do you agree with _____?" Probe for information: facts, opinions, and impressions.

- **Keep on track.** Encourage good discussion, but don't be timid about calling time on a given question and moving ahead. Part of your job is clock management. If the group decides to spend extra time on a given question or activity, consider skipping or spending less time on a later question or activity in order to stay on schedule.

- **Know that building "group trust" takes time.** While you want to do the best job you can to lead and facilitate, avoid setting unrealistic expectations. Take what you get and build from there. Build on strengths of members and affirm their responses.

- **Enjoy the process.** Enjoy learning and growing with your group.

The good news is that it isn't all up to you! As a person who is gifted for this ministry, you can trust the Holy Spirit to be at work through your leadership to accomplish God's purpose in the lives of your group members. In fact, you can expect surprising discoveries along the way!

INTRODUCTORY SESSION OR PASTOR'S COFFEE
WHAT DOES IT MEAN TO BE A UNITED METHODIST?
(Recommended but optional)

An introductory session or pastor's coffee is a great way to kick off *A Disciple's Path*. In either case, the material covered is essentially the same. An introductory session is the logical choice for established groups or members seeking to grow in their understanding and application of discipleship from a uniquely Wesleyan perspective. A pastor's coffee is more appropriate for prospective or new members and includes coffee and refreshments as well as the participation of the pastor(s).

Generally speaking, the purpose of a pastor's coffee is to provide guests, newcomers, and those interested in joining the church the opportunity to meet the pastor(s), ask any questions they might have, discover the ways in which to engage in the life of the church, and learn what church membership means. Because this pastor's coffee precedes a six-week study of discipleship in the United Methodist tradition, it also includes a brief overview of the history, beliefs, and practices of The United Methodist Church as well as the mission, values, strategy, and vision of your local church (a customizable template is provided on the CD-ROM).

In light of the unique nature and purpose of this introductory session/pastor's coffee, the format and suggested time allotments for the session vary slightly from those of sessions 1-6.

Preparation

- Have participants register in advance for the introductory session or pastor's coffee. Sample reminder e-mails are included on the CD-ROM.

- For a pastor's coffee, consider recruiting and training a volunteer to coordinate and host the coffee. The volunteer can help to prepare and distribute participant folders (see below), prepare the room, coordinate the sign-in process, and oversee refreshments and coffee.

- In advance of either a pastor's coffee or introductory session, prepare a folder for each participant that includes the following materials from the CD-ROM. ***Note:*** *Several of these items are samples or templates that can be customized or adapted for your congregation's needs.*

Left Side of Folder:
- Next Steps Card (pastor's coffee only)
- A Disciple's Path Class Covenant
- What Church Membership Means

Note: *For a pastor's coffee, you also may want to include a copy of your most recent church newsletter or other informational materials specific to your congregation.*

Right Side of Folder:
- Church History Tree
- United Methodist Church History Flowchart
- United Methodist Church Structure and Organization
- Introduction to The United Methodist Church: History, Structure, and Beliefs
- Mission, Values, Strategy, and Vision—Sample (adapt for your church)

• Print copies of the Personal Information Form (recommended for pastor's coffee; can be modified for introductory session *if desired*) and the Sign-in Sheet provided on the CD-ROM (versions provided for a pastor's coffee and group session).

• Prepare name tags or tent cards.

• **For an introductory session:** Have copies of the *Daily Workbook* and *Companion Reader* available and ready to distribute. At the end of the session, instruct participants to read and complete Week 1 in the *Daily Workbook* and through Chapter 1 in the *Companion Reader* prior to Session 1.

• **For a pastor's coffee:** You have the option of distributing books at this time or allowing attendees to decide if they would like to sign up for *A Disciple's Path* (see the Next Steps Card included on the CD-ROM). If you choose the first option, instruct participants to read and complete Week 1 in the *Daily Workbook* and through chapter 1 in the *Companion Reader* prior to Session 1. If you choose the latter option, send a follow-up e-mail to those who sign up for *A Disciple's Path* (see sample e-mail on the CD-

ROM), indicating where and when to obtain books and how to prepare for Session 1.

• Review the Introductory Session PowerPoint on the CD-ROM. Also review "Why Are You a United Methodist?" in the *Companion Reader* and "What It Means to Be a United Methodist" in the *Daily Workbook*.

• If you are using the PowerPoint presentation, be sure the projection equipment and screen are in the room and in working order before the session begins.

Note: *Slide numbers throughout this outline refer to the PowerPoint presentation for the session if you choose to use it.*

Welcome / Sign-in (5-7 minutes)

• Have participants sign in and provide their e-mail address and primary phone number (slide 1).

• Give each participant a name tag or tent card, prepared folder, and Personal Information Form (optional for introductory session). Have participants complete and return the form.

• Provide copies of the *Daily Workbook* and *Companion Reader*, unless you have decided to make these available at another time prior to Session 1.

• If you are having a pastor's coffee, allow time for participants to get coffee and refreshments and mingle.

Objectives (2 minutes)

- Introduce yourself (and any other leaders/staff members attending) and review the objectives of this session (slide 2). Participants will:
  - Get to know others in the group.
  - Understand the basic rhythm and expectations of the six-week study *A Disciple's Path*.
  - Review United Methodist history, beliefs, organization, and structure.
  - Understand this congregation's mission, values, strategy, and vision.
  - Learn what church membership means.
  - Ask questions.

- Provide dates and times for *A Disciple's Path* group sessions as well as other housekeeping items (slide 3). Customize the slide for your class schedule.

- Briefly walk through the *Daily Workbook*, pointing out what a daily reading looks like and what is involved in completing the activities and questions (less than 30 minutes per day). Introduce the *Companion Reader* as a valuable tool for weekly reading and study (slide 4).

Opening Prayer (1 minute)

Read the following prayer in unison or offer a spontaneous prayer (slide 5):

Gracious and Loving God, we gather as your people to explore, to learn, to understand more about you and who you call us to become. Open our minds and hearts to receive your gift of grace.

Open our mouths and hands to offer your grace to others. In the name of Jesus the Christ we pray. Amen.

Introductions (15 minutes)

- Ask participants to share their names, the faith tradition or denomination in which they were raised, three facts about themselves (this can be anything they want to share about themselves, including how they found their way to this church), and one question they bring with them about what it means to be part of this congregation (slide 6). If you are not using the PowerPoint presentation, write the list on a board or chart to help participants remember what to share:
  - Name
  - Faith tradition / denomination
  - 3 facts about yourself
  - 1 question about the church or class

- Set the example by going first, giving a brief response.

- As participants share their questions, have someone record them. Make sure that every question is answered by the end of the session.

Note: If you have fewer than ten people, do the introductions together. If your group is larger than ten people, you may want to break into small groups for sharing in order to keep things moving.

Orientation (25 minutes)

Present the following material according to the Introductory Session PowerPoint presentation or using the materials provided in the participant folder. Instruct participants to take the pages out of their folders and follow along.

Share Class Objectives

- Learn the discipleship pathway and how to grow your faith in this congregation.

- Experience the daily rhythm of reading scripture and journaling.

- Discover your spiritual gift.

- Identify a group or class that meets your next step along the discipleship journey.

- Talk with someone to find a place to serve in ministry.

- Make an informed decision about your next step on the discipleship pathway. (slide 7)

Church History, Structure, and Beliefs

- Review the Church History Tree Diagram (slide 8). Invite persons who have had experience in one or more different faith traditions or denominations to identity the branch or branches on which they grew up, were baptized, or found faith in Christ.

- Review The United Methodist Church History Flowchart (slide 9).

- Review Introduction to The United Methodist Church: History, Beliefs, and Structure (slides 10-15). Show The UMC: Organization & Structure (slide 11) when talking about the structure of the church. Explain that General Conference is the only entity that can speak for The United Methodist Church. Before moving on to slide 16, bring attention to the list of recommended resources on the Introduction to The United Methodist Church handout, or consider having these and other resources available for those who want to know more (see www.cokesbury.com):
  - Thomas S. McNally's *Questions and Answers About The United Methodist Church*, Abingdon Press, 1995
  - Belton Joyner's *The "Unofficial" United Methodist Handbook*, Abingdon Press, 2007
  - Introductory brochures on Communion and United Methodists, Baptism and United Methodists, It's All About God's Grace, Membership and United Methodists, The People of The United Methodist Church, and What's So Great about Being United Methodist?
  - http://UMC.org
  - http://gbod.org

Local Church Mission, Vision, Strategy, and Values

- Ask if anyone knows your congregation's mission (slide 16).

- Provide the history of your local congregation and your church's mission, core values, vision, and strategic objectives or goals (slides 17-20). If you do not already have printed materials, customize the handouts on the CD-ROM. If using the PowerPoint presentation, customize the slides on Mission, Core Values, Vision, and Strategy for your church, or delete these slides and use printed materials only.

What Church Membership Means

- Review what church membership means (slide 21).

- Introduce the vows that each person makes when becoming a member of The United Methodist Church and the corresponding spiritual practices that enable us to fulfill these vows. These vows and practices form the foundation for the rest of the class sessions (slides 22-27).
  - **Prayer:** *Prayer and Scripture Meditation.* Spending time in prayer each day, and studying and reflecting on the Bible to experience the living Word of hope in the written word of Scripture.
  - **Presence:** *Corporate Worship and Small-group Community.* Celebrating God's presence in worship with a faith community, and experiencing Christian community in a small group to pray, learn, and grow together.
  - **Gifts:** *Financial Generosity.* Practicing Christian stewardship through the biblical discipline of tithing.
  - **Service:** *Spiritual Gifts and Gifts-based Service.* Discovering our spiritual gifts and participating in God's work through the ministry of the church.
  - **Witness:** *Invitational Evangelism.* Inviting others to experience God's love and become disciples of Jesus Christ.

A Disciple's Path *Class Covenant*

- Review the class covenant (slide 28). If you are having a pastor's coffee and participants have not yet signed up for *A Disciple's Path*, take this opportunity to describe the class.

- Present the three basic rules:
  1. **Be on time** so we can achieve the session's objectives.
  2. **Complete the readings and activities** and come prepared. If you don't participate, you'll get so much less out of it. So will everyone else!
  3. **Contact us if you are unable to attend class.** If you know you will miss more than one session, let's discuss if there may be a better time for you to take this class.

- (Pastor's Coffee Only) Instruct participants to take the Next Steps Card from their folder, fill it out, and return it to you. (Customize the sample on the CD-ROM for your congregation.)

Wrap Up / Looking Ahead to Next Week (5 minutes)

- Refer back to the list of questions that participants shared during the introduction. Answer any questions that have not been answered. Check in with the group to see if there are additional questions (slide 29).

- Tell participants that their daily reading and next week's group session will focus on A Disciple's Path Defined. Instruct them to read the introduction and complete Week 1 in the *Daily Workbook* and read the introduction and chapter 1 in the *Companion Reader* before the next session. Emphasize that completing the material in the *Daily Workbook* will enrich the group session for everyone (slide 30).

Take-home Message and Closing Prayer (5 minutes)

- Have the participants stand in a circle. Ask each participant to think about what was his or her "take home" message—the one thing that spoke most loudly or clearly from today's session. Allow a few people to respond (slide 31).

- Say a closing prayer—the one below or one of your own. If you wish, ask for a volunteer who will lead the opening and closing prayers during Session 1.

O God, we thank you for calling us to be disciples of Jesus Christ. As we begin this journey, we pray that your Spirit will guide us as we discover what it will mean to live as growing disciples in the life of this congregation. Amen.

Note: *If this is a pastor's coffee or introductory session for prospective or new members, consider scheduling a tour of the church facilities after class.*

Session 1
A Disciple's Path Defined

Note: Some introductory material is included in the session outline for those groups that chose not to have an introductory session or pastor's coffee. If you had an introductory session or pastor's coffee, you may skip this material. If you plan to include this material, it will add five to ten minutes of class time. If this presents a problem, simply reduce the amount of time you spend on one of the other segments, such as the Daily Workbook *Discussion.*

Preparation

- Review the framework of *A Disciple's Path* by reading the Introduction and Week 1 in the *Daily Workbook*.

- Read the introduction and chapter 1 in the *Companion Reader*. This will be review if you had an introductory session.

- Read the Scripture passages assigned for the week:
  - Day 1: Luke 10:27; Mark 12:29-34; Galatians 5:14; 1 Corinthians 13:13; John 13:35
  - Day 2: John 1:43-51; 1 John 1:5-7; Psalm 119:1-5, 57-60, 105
  - Day 3: Ephesians 1:15-23; 3:14-20; Colossians 2:6-7
  - Day 4: 1 Timothy 4:6-16; 2 Timothy 1:1-7; Philippians 2:1-18; Hebrews 10:19-25
  - Day 5: 1 Corinthians 9:24-25; Romans 12:1-21

- Review the Session 1 PowerPoint found on the CD-ROM prior to class and be prepared to walk the class through the presentation (if you choose to utilize this resource).

Note: Notes and talking points related to the discipleship path are on the PowerPoint notes pages. This PowerPoint presentation is your guide for the session, and you may choose to print and distribute hard copies of the presentation.

- Prepare copies of the following handouts found on the CD-ROM for each member of the class:
  - Session 1 PowerPoint in handout style (if you choose to distribute this resource)
  - Mind Mapping Guidelines (if you choose to do this optional activity)

Sign-in / Objectives
(2 minutes)

Note: Slide numbers throughout this session outline refer to the PowerPoint presentation for Session 1, if you choose to use it.

- Invite participants to sign in and make a nametag. If the group is smaller and seated around a table, tent cards are another option for names (slide 1).

- If you did *not* have an introductory session/pastor's coffee, allow a few additional minutes to:
  - Have participants provide e-mail address and phone number(s) as they sign in.
  - Distribute copies of the *Daily Workbook* and *Companion Reader* (if you have not already done so). Explain that there are five days of readings and home activities for each week, which may be completed in about thirty minutes per day.
  - Provide the dates and times for the group sessions and review any other housekeeping items.
  - Cover the class objectives (slide 2).
    1. Learn the discipleship pathway and how to grow your faith in this congregation.
    2. Experience the daily rhythm of reading scripture and journaling.
    3. Discover your spiritual gift.
    4. Identify a group or class that meets your next step along the discipleship journey.
    5. Talk with someone to find a place to serve in ministry.
    6. Make an informed decision about your next step on the discipleship pathway.

  - Present three basic rules: (slide 3)
    1. **Be on time** so we can achieve the session's objectives.
    2. **Complete the readings and activities** and come prepared. If you don't participate, you'll get so much less out of it. So will everyone else!
    3. **Contact us if you are unable to attend class.** If you know you will miss more than one session, let's discuss if there may be a better time for you to take this class.

- Share the objectives of the session (slide 4):
  1. Understand the basic rhythm and expectations of the class.
  2. Understand the discipleship path.
  3. Understand grace in the Wesleyan tradition.
  4. Assess where you are in your relationship to Christ.
  5. Review the spiritual practices that stimulate growth.

Note: As group leader, you should complete the daily readings and workbook activities (about 30 minutes per day); bring your notes and questions to class each week; actively participate in class discussions; listen to, learn from, and share with one another.

Introductions and Overview
(5 minutes)

Note: Skip this segment if you had an introductory session/pastor's coffee.

If you did not have an introductory class or pastor's coffee:

- Ask participants to introduce themselves by giving their names and their hopes for the class/group. As participants share, record their answers on the board.

Note: If you have fewer than ten people, do the introductions together. If your group is larger than ten people, you may want to break into small groups for sharing in order to keep things moving.

Opening Prayer (1 minute)

- Explain that you will open and close each session with prayer and scripture.

- Read the following prayer, offer a spontaneous prayer, or invite a participant to pray (slide 5).

Thanks be to Thee, my Lord Jesus Christ
For all the benefits Thou hast given me,
For all the pains and insults Thou hast borne
  for me.
O most merciful Redeemer, friend and brother,
May I know Thee more clearly,
Love Thee more dearly,
Follow Thee more nearly.[1]
　　　　　—St. Richard of Chichester (1197-1253)

Biblical Foundation (2 minutes)

- Read Luke 10:25-28 (slide 6).

Note: Read the passage yourself or invite a group member to read it.

- Provide a brief summary of the passage. *Example:* This passage highlights that we are to love God and love others. Jesus said, "Do this and you will live." That is what this study is designed to help us discover: how to inherit salvation in the Wesleyan tradition and live.

- Suggested talking points:
  - "You will live"—That's why we are here: to learn to live more abundantly through

following Jesus in the United Methodist tradition. Today we'll be talking about what it means to be a disciple of Jesus and how to grow in our spiritual journey—to deepen our love for God and our love for others.
  - We'll be spending time in the Bible each week, so please bring yours with you next week. If you don't have one, we can help you select one; you will be reading about Bible translations this week.

Daily Workbook Discussion
(45 minutes for 60-minute session; 55 minutes for 90-minute session)

Work through the following outline, using the interactive elements as they are presented, or follow the PowerPoint presentation. If participants received their books prior to this session, invite them to refer to the notes, responses, and questions they recorded through the week as the discussion progresses.

1. What does the word *disciple* mean to you? (slide 7)

Disciple means "pupil," "apprentice," or "adherent." See Latin *discipulus* (pupil); from *discipere* "to grasp intellectually, analyze thoroughly," *dis* (apart) + *capere* (to take, grasp, comprehend).[2]

2. Focus on the words of Jesus in Luke 10:25-28. What do his words mean for you? (slide 8)

- Suggested talking points:
  - Most people today think of themselves as being on a spiritual journey. Even if they are not Christians, they have ideas and beliefs that guide them. As Christians, we want to be clear about our faith journey so that we know what we should be doing to make progress and so that we can more easily share our faith story with others.
  - Remember the Good Samaritan story in Luke? The setup to that story is today's passage; an expert in the law asks Jesus, "What must I do to inherit eternal life?" Jesus asks in return what is written in the law. The man answers, "Love the Lord your God with all your heart and with all your soul and with all your strength and with all your mind; and love your neighbor as yourself." Jesus replies, "You have answered correctly, do this and you will live."
  - So our question becomes, How do we do this? *A Disciple's Path* attempts to answer this question.

Five Essentials of the Discipleship Pathway

- Review the five essentials of the disciple's path (slide 9):
  1. Understand the definition of *disciple*.
  2. Learn the relationship stages of growth.
  3. Understand grace and God's role, the church's role, and your role in spiritual growth.
  4. Recognize that spiritual practices are what grow our relationship with God, and that they look different as we grow.
  5. Join with the church to participate in God's transformation of the world.

Definition of a Disciple

- Remind participants that this was covered in Day 1 of their reading in the *Daily Workbook* (page 16). If participants have just received their books, give them a minute or so to write down a definition.

- Have participants turn to someone next to them and share their definition.

- Invite sharing from the group. Note similarities and differences. Point out that our understanding of what a disciple is shapes how we attempt to form, grow, and send disciples into the world.

- Give a brief overview of how *A Disciple's Path* defines a disciple (slide 10; Day 1 in the *Daily Workbook*):
  - "A follower of Jesus"—one who trusts Jesus for personal salvation and for bringing healing and wholeness to the world.
  - ". . . whose life is centering"—one who continues to grow spiritually throughout life.
  - ". . . on loving God and loving others"—one who loves God and obeys Jesus' command to love one another (see John 13:35).

- Suggested talking points:
  - First, we must define what we mean by the word *disciple*. Different churches define a disciple different ways. We chose this definition: A follower of Jesus whose life is centering on loving God and loving others. So, what does this mean?
  - As Christians, we want to ground the definition in following Jesus. What does it

mean to follow Jesus? It suggests that you are attracted to Jesus and his teaching. It also suggests you believe who he, and the church, says he was and that you are willing to trust him for your personal salvation. There are other beliefs, such as those contained in the Apostle's Creed, that some would say are essential, but for now we will just focus on belief "in Jesus."

○ But is belief enough to be considered a "follower of Jesus"? The word *follow* implies something that is done with your feet, not just your head. Action is required in order to be a follower of Jesus. What kind of action are we talking about? The Gospels tell us in three different places that the greatest commandment is to love God with all your heart, soul, strength, and mind and the second is like it: love your neighbor as yourself (Matthew 22:39; Mark 12:31; Luke 10:25-28). Based on this, we have described this action as loving God and loving others. In other words, a disciple is one who makes God's love real in the world.

○ The really interesting thing about trying to link belief and action is that they don't really ever change at the same time. But when they are put together, the miracle of transformation happens. Sometimes belief is enough to change action; sometimes action happens first, and then we figure out what we think about it. But when we understand what we believe and live out those beliefs by loving God and loving others, we are really followers of Jesus, whose lives are centering on loving God and loving others.

○ Being a disciple is essentially about being in relationship with Jesus. So, let's look at how this relationship changes as we are transformed.

Stages of Relationship

• Review the stages of relationship: Ignoring, Exploring, Getting Started, Going Deeper, Centering (slide 11; Day 2 in the *Daily Workbook*).

• Suggested talking points:
  ○ One way to look at spiritual growth is how people at different stages of their faith might describe their relationship with Jesus. We have used broad categorizes for these stages. Another way to look at this would be in terms of our relationship with God, growing from strangers to acquaintances, friends, good friends, and intimate friends. These are broad categories, but they give us an idea of what our relationship with Jesus might look like as we grow in faith. These stages are not rigid in nature but flexible and fluid. The faith journey, like any journey, is filled with twists and turns.
  ○ Consider your reflections on the readings and share (in pairs, if the group is large) where you see yourself in relationship with God at this point in your journey.
  ○ Knowing where we see ourselves now helps us begin to identify next

steps as we continually grow and move more deeply into living a Christ-centered life.

○ What helps us grow in this relationship? How do we move from exploring to centering on Christ?

Roles and Responsibilities

- Suggested talking points (slide 12; Day 3 in the *Daily Workbook*):
  ○ The good news is that it is not up to us to do this alone! God, the church, and each one of us has a role to play, and all of these roles interact and work together to help us grow as disciples.
  ○ If we look at the Wesleyan theology for becoming a disciple, we find that Christian faith formation occurs through the partnership of God's action and human action. God's grace works within persons to deepen their relationship with Jesus through the instruction, nurture, and care of the faith community, leading them to respond to the enabling work of the Holy Spirit in faithful Christian discipleship.
  ○ Growth in faith occurs not just through religious instruction or religious experience but through a combination of influences—such as worship, witness, study, prayer, service, and fellowship—that shape our faith through participation in the life of the church.
  ○ All three cogs of the wheel are required. God does God's part, but we have a responsibility to respond and to put our faith into practice; and

the church has a responsibility to provide experiences and opportunities for people to engage with and to nurture people as they seek to grow.

The Three Roles

1) God's Role through Grace

- Explain prevenient, justifying, and sanctifying grace, pointing out how they overlay the relationship stages (slide 13; Day 3 in the *Daily Workbook*).

- Suggested talking points:
  ○ If we look first at God's role in this process, we find that God is at work in our lives in different ways as we grow in our faith. John Wesley described this as God's grace that is shown to us in three different ways.
  ○ *Prevenient grace* means that God meets us where we are, before we have made any decision to follow God. It exists prior to and without reference to anything we may have done. God is calling all persons into relationship, and we can choose how we will respond. Some of us will ignore this call.
  ○ If we choose to become disciples of Christ, we are "justified" by grace. *Justifying grace* is offered by God to all people; we receive it by faith and trust in Christ, through whom God pardons us of sin. This justifying grace cancels our guilt and empowers us to resist the power of sin and to fully love God and neighbor.

Wesley believed that justification occurs in different ways for different people. It may happen in one transforming moment, as in response to an altar call, or it may involve a series of decisions across time.

○ But, we are never done. We continue to work out our salvation as we grow in faith. Through *sanctifying grace* we learn that it is not "all about me," and we participate in God's redemption of the world. Sanctifying grace sustains disciples on the journey toward perfection of love: genuine love for God with heart, soul, mind, and strength, and love for our neighbors as for ourselves.

2) The Roles of Church and Family

• Explain that the church's and family's roles are to nurture, encourage, and challenge us as we grow; in the church, this is primarily done by providing opportunities to experience God in Christian community through small groups, corporate worship, and opportunities to use our spiritual gifts in service (slide 14; Day 4 in the *Daily Workbook*).

3) The Role of Each Individual

• Suggested talking points (slide 15; Day 5 in the *Daily Workbook*):
○ National research found that many people rely on church programs as their only way to grow spiritually. These programs help, but God also uses personal spiritual disciplines to grow us in the likeness and image of Jesus.

○ So this is how we put our faith into action. First, we take advantage of the opportunities given to us by the church.
○ But we can't just show up at church every time the doors are open and think that we will grow spiritually. In addition to attending worship and being involved in a small group and some kind of service role or ministry, we each have a responsibility to be engaged in the practice of personal spiritual disciplines. The Methodist tradition believes that God uses our practice of spiritual disciplines to shape us in Christ's image. There are many spiritual disciplines, but those we lift up in *A Disciple's Path* are the essential ones that are catalytic to spiritual growth.

• Note that spiritual practices change as we grow. They don't remain the same.

Putting It Together

• Suggested talking points (slides 16-19):
○ If we begin to put all of these roles together, this is what it looks like. We said that God is responsible for all spiritual growth. God calls us into relationship with Jesus, and we respond. As we follow and grow in the spiritual practices (both as individuals and as a faith community), God moves us more deeply into loving God and loving others. To put it another way, as we follow Jesus and move to a life

that is centering in loving God and loving others through our beliefs and actions (the arrows pointing in), God transforms our hearts. (slide 16)

○ Transformed hearts will always result in lives that are focused outwardly and are actively involved in God's transformation of the world (the arrows pointing out). This always becomes bigger than you and what you could do on your own. Spiritual growth is never just about you; it has an impact on the whole church. This happens both individually and communally. When the whole community is growing together, amazing things happen. (slide 17)

○ God uses our response in God's redeeming work, and miracles happen. As we all grow together, lives are transformed, Christian community is created, and the surrounding community and the world are healed. This is all part of God's plan of salvation and redemption, and each one of us has an important part to play. Why does this matter? (slide 18)

○ We believe this is God's vision—that as we all faithfully do our part, individually and as a faith community, the Holy Spirit will transform lives, creating Christian community and healing the neighborhood, the larger community, and the world.

○ We also believe this is God's plan for the church, and God's plan for our lives is better than any we might create.

○ So, what is your next step?

○ Spiritual practices are an expression of loving God and others. God changes us through these practices, and as we change, the ways in which we practice these disciplines will also change. This chart offers one idea of how these practices might change. You may develop your own chart to record your journey along the discipleship pathway. (slide 19)

○ Growth in one discipline does not necessarily correspond with growth in other areas. You can be exploring one practice and going deeper in another. And of course, growth in these practices does not necessarily correspond with growth in our beliefs. Sometimes we change our belief, and one of these practices changes as a result. Other times, we begin with changing our actions, and through the practice of these spiritual disciplines our beliefs are changed. Once again, growth is not ever as linear as this table indicates. The discipleship pathway is seldom a straight line, and there will be times of regression. It is a true path nevertheless, and the important thing is to keep following Jesus down the path. Wherever you are right now is great, but one thing is certain: it is not where you are supposed to stay indefinitely. God is never through with us.

○ So, think about where you are and what your next step could be to make God's love real in the world.

• Have participants turn to page 30 in the *Daily Workbook* and refer to their notes or write notes regarding their current practice of the spiritual disciplines, both individually and corporately (in community).

Session Summary

- The definition of a disciple focuses on heart transformation through belief and action.

- There are stages of growth. We grow deeper in relationship, mirroring a human relationship's development from strangers to intimate friends.

- God, the church and family, and the individual all have roles to play in growing faith.
  - God calls us into loving relationship through grace.
  - The church's role is to provide opportunities to experience God in Christian community.
  - The individual's role is to respond to God's grace by participating in the life of the church AND to practice personal spiritual disciplines, which move us into deeper relationship with Christ and grow our love for God and others.

- All of these practices look different as we grow.

- Wherever we are now is okay, but we have the opportunity to deepen our relationship (through belief and action), and God wants us to grow. The point is movement and growth!
(slide 20)

Optional Activity (20 minutes, 90-minute session only)

- Create individual charts or maps of spiritual growth, following the spiritual practices chart (slide 19, page 29 in the *Daily Workbook*) as a guide. You might use a timeline or mind map format.
  - Timeline: a horizontal line represents birth to today; note significant moments, people, or events that contributed to your spiritual growth and note how your spiritual practices changed and developed as a result.
  - Mind map: Begin with a central statement about or picture of spiritual perfection. Draw or record spiritual practices in relation to this central image and connect them as appropriate. For more information on mind mapping, see Mind Mapping Guidelines on the CD-ROM. Consider providing this as a handout guide.

Looking Ahead To Next Week (5 minutes)

- Tell participants that next week's focus is Prayers: Prayer and Scripture Meditation (slide 21).

- Instruct participants to complete Week 2 in the *Daily Workbook* and read chapter 2 in the *Companion Reader* before the next session. Emphasize that completing the material will enrich the next session for everyone.

- Remind participants to bring their Bibles to class next week.

- Ask if there are any questions.

Take-home Message and Closing Prayer (5 minutes)

- Have participants stand in a circle. Ask each participant to share his or her "take home" message—the one thing that spoke most loudly or clearly from today's session (slide 22).

- Offer a closing prayer—the one below or a spontaneous prayer of your own. Consider asking for a volunteer to lead opening and closing prayers next week.

Gracious and loving God, our journey of discovery has begun. We are grateful for your presence among us and within us as we have shared and learned from one another. We ask that you continue to be with each member of this group as we move through the coming week—working, playing, studying, and praying—until we come together again to deepen our understanding of the discipleship path and how to travel it together. Amen.

***Note:** If this is a new member class and you did not have an introductory session or pastor's coffee, consider scheduling a tour of the church facilities after class.*

Session 2
Prayers: Prayer and Scripture Meditation

Preparation

- Complete the readings and questions for Week 2 in the *Daily Workbook* and read chapter 2 in the *Companion Reader*. Highlight selections from the *Companion Reader* that you feel are particularly helpful for this week's lesson.

- Read the Scripture passages assigned for the week:
  - Day 1: Luke 11:1-4; Matthew 6:9-14
  - Day 2: Philippians 4:4-7; Psalm 139:23-24; Luke 18:9-14
  - Day 3: Psalm 119:97-105, 129-133; 2 Timothy 3:10-17
  - Day 4: Matthew 7:24-27; 13:51-53; 2 Timothy 1:11-12
  - Day 5: Luke 11:34; Mark 12:28-34; John 1:1-15

- Prepare copies of the following handouts found on the CD-ROM for each member of the class:
  - Who Said That? Bible Quiz (if you are doing the optional activity)
  - Small-group Overview (Session 3 folder; adapt the template for your congregation)

- Have available at least one Bible dictionary and one Bible concordance to illustrate helpful Bible study tools. If your church library does not include these reference resources, ask your pastor to help you locate them.

Sign-in / Objectives (2 minutes)

- Invite participants to sign in and make a nametag. If the group is smaller and seated around a table, tent cards are another option for names.
- Share the objectives of the session. Participants will:
  1. Understand and discuss prayer and some prayer methods.
  2. Learn how to get to know the Bible.
  3. Understand the Wesleyan Quadrilateral.
  4. Explore an overview of the Bible and understand how it forms us.
  5. Assess where they can grow in Bible study/reflection.
  6. Learn SOAPY and *Lectio Divina*.

Opening Prayer (1 minute)

- Say the Lord's Prayer together. Use the text from #895 in *The United Methodist Hymnal* or whichever version your church uses on a regular basis.

Biblical Foundation (2 minutes)

- Read Matthew 6:5-15.

Note: Read the passage yourself or invite a group member to read it.

- Provide a brief summary of the passage. Jesus gives instruction on prayer in Matthew's version of the Lord's Prayer.

- Suggested talking points:
  - This Scripture passage highlights some of what Jesus said about prayer.
  - It calls us to private prayer. It is not a condemnation of public or shared prayer, but it condemns those who pray publicly to show how pious they are.
  - Jesus calls us to authentic prayer because God desires relationship with us. Prayer and Scripture reflection deepen our relationship with God and raise our awareness of God's presence in our lives.

Daily Workbook Discussion
(45 minutes for 60-minute session; 55 minutes for 90-minute session)

Work through the following outline, using the interactive elements as they are presented. Invite the class members to refer to the notes, responses, and questions they recorded through the week as the discussion progresses.

Understand and Discuss Prayer and Several Prayer Methods

- ACTS (Adoration, Confession, Thanksgiving, Supplication)
  - Ask if anyone would like to share the ACTS prayer he or she wrote in the *Daily Workbook* (page 36). Be prepared to share your own prayer, if no one volunteers.

> "Wesley knew that a life of prayer was not an accident or a natural consequence of just living. He was convinced that a life of prayer was the result of a determined and disciplined effort. . . . Without this disciplined effort, prayer would become secondary and our relationship with God left to suffocate under the cares and delights of the world."[3]
> —Rueben Job

- Five-finger prayer
  - Ask if anyone who wrote or tried a five-finger prayer during the week would be willing to share it with the class (*Daily Workbook,* page 36).

- Jesus prayer (Luke 18:13)
  - "Lord Jesus Christ, have mercy on me, a sinner." It also can be shortened to "Lord, have mercy" or "Jesus, have mercy."
  - Ask if anyone would like to share responses to the reflection questions on the Jesus prayer (*Daily Workbook,* page 37).

- Our practice of prayer
  - Lead a discussion on the current prayer practice of class members. How do they pray,

where, and how often? How satisfied are they with their current prayer practice? What would they like to see changed or improved? How can the class work together on these goals?

Learn How to Get to Know the Bible

- Invite class members to share what version of the Bible they have and why they chose it or how they acquired it.

- Review the helpful tips for reading and studying the Bible (*Daily Workbook* pages 39-40).

- Offer this additional information about the Bible:
  ○ There are 66 books in the Protestant Bible: 39 in the Old Testament, 27 in the New Testament.
  ○ Some translations may also include a section called "the Apocrypha" between the Old and New Testaments. These writings are included in the canon of the Roman Catholic Scriptures but are not included in most Protestant collections. The Protestant Reformers considered them to be written by godly men, but not necessarily inspired by God. They were considered appropriate and helpful to read, but not for inclusion in the Holy Scripture.
  ○ The Bible is a community book that emerged out of the experience of a people of faith, the inspired record of the people who experienced the active word of God. *Inspired* doesn't mean that God dictated text to passive notetakers. It means that God's presence was breathed into it and God's truth is at the central core.
  ○ The central affirmation of the Bible is that Jesus is God's word made flesh, God's self-revelation in human form.
  ○ We are to keep our eyes on the big story of God's saving action in human history. The world is broken and bruised, and the way God chooses to save and redeem the world is through divine grace and the self-giving love of Jesus (that is THE big story).
  ○ "The Bible . . . is rooted in historically verifiable events, but its truth goes beyond anything that can be proved by the scientific method. It's true in the way it claims to be true, namely, in telling us the story of God's relationship with God's creation. It touches the deepest truth of your life and mine, revealing the truth about who God is and what God intends for us" (*Companion Reader*, page 33).

- Point out that the most effective way to hear the word of God is to be involved in a small group, sharing diverse approaches to the text and interpretations of it.

Understand the Wesleyan Quadrilateral

Scripture, Tradition, Reason, Experience

- Invite class members to share responses to the reflection questions found on page 44 in the *Daily Workbook*. How do they employ the elements of the Quadrilateral in making decisions and growing in their faith?

- Ask participants if they feel that one way is superior to or "more correct" than another, and if so, why? Take this opportunity to offer a word of grace about embracing a diversity of approaches to deepening our relationship with God and one another. For some people, Scripture is the beginning and end of knowing God. Others may put more emphasis on their personal experience of God. Invite the class to share the value they perceive in making use of all four elements of the quadrilateral for balance and harmony in community.

- Explain that when we undertake prayer and Scripture study as spiritual disciplines, we make room for the Holy Spirit to work in our lives, opening us to new possibilities in service and relationship. We make space for God to "read us" through authentic encounter in listening and study.

Learn SOAPY

- Explain that SOAPY is a method of Bible reflection through Scripture, Observation, Application, Prayer, and Yield. The SOAPY explanation and example in the *Daily Workbook* are adapted from the Life Journal website of United Methodist Bishop Dick Wills and are based on the teaching of Wayne Cordeiro of New Hope Christian Fellowship in Honolulu.

- Ask if anyone is willing to share the lessons learned from applying the SOAPY method to Mark 12:28-34 (*Daily Workbook*, page 47).
- Invite everyone to share what the experience was like for them and what value they found in studying Scripture in this way. What was new? What was surprising? What was uncomfortable and why?
- Be sure the class has the web address for the Life Journal (www.nashvilleareajournal.org), and encourage them to explore the site, which offers the Online Life Journal with daily Scripture readings that guide the reader through the Bible in a year.

Learn Lectio Divina

- Introduce *Lectio Divina* (Divine Reading; pronounced lektīō dĭvīn), an ancient practice of contemplative Bible study through *Lectio*, Meditation, *Oratio* (ôrätīō), Contemplation.
- Ask if anyone is willing to share the lessons learned from studying John 1:1-15 using the practice of *Lectio Divina* (*Daily Workbook*, page 47).
- Invite participants to share what the experience was like for them and what value they found in studying Scripture in this way. What was new? What was surprising? What was uncomfortable and why?

Optional Activity (20 minutes, 90-minute session only)

- Distribute copies of Who Said That? Bible Quiz and provide 10 minutes for class members to complete it. Instruct them to use any tools available to them in their own Bibles or in the Bible dictionary and Bible concordance you have provided. Class members who have access to the Internet may also use online tools such as Bible.Oremus.org, Crosswalk.com, or BibleGateway.com. If access to the Internet is not available, be sure to inform them of these tools for use at home.
  - At the end of 10 minutes, invite participants to share their answers. Provide answers for any missed items, and ask what they learned from the experience of searching for passages in this way.
  - Focus on the exercise as a means for getting to know the Bible, not as a competition. You might, however, want to provide a small gift, perhaps a bookmark, to anyone who answered all of the questions correctly.

Looking Ahead to Next Week
(5 minutes)

- Choose prayer partners within the group. This can be done by writing each person's name on a slip of paper and having class members choose one from a basket. Obviously, if they get their own names, they should put the slip back. Each person should commit to daily prayer that includes prayer partners.

- Tell participants that next week's focus is Presence: Corporate Worship and Small-group Community. Instruct them to complete Week 3 in the *Daily Workbook* and read chapter 3 in the *Companion Reader* before the next session. Emphasize that completing the material in the *Daily Workbook* will enrich the next session for everyone.

- To provide a reference list of small-group options available in your congregation, customize the Small-group Overview on the CD-ROM and distribute copies. Explain that this listing will help them as they complete the Small-group Profile in the *Daily Workbook* before the next session. Instruct them to bring the Small-group Overview with them to the next session so that they may complete and turn in the top portion for follow-up with the group or individuals charged with connecting members to the life of the church.

- Ask if there are any questions.

Take-home Message and Closing Prayer
(5 minutes)

- Stand in a circle.

- Ask each participant to share his or her "take home" message—the one thing that spoke most loudly or clearly from today's session.

- Offer a closing prayer—the one below or a spontaneous prayer of your own. Consider asking for a volunteer to lead opening and closing prayers next week.

Gracious and loving God, we are grateful for your presence among us and within us as we have shared and learned from one another. We ask that you continue to be with each member of this group as we move through the coming week—working, playing, studying, and praying—until we come together again to deepen our understanding of the discipleship path and how to travel it together. Amen.

Session 3
Presence: Corporate Worship and Small-group Community

Preparation

- Complete the readings and questions for Week 3 in the *Daily Workbook* and read chapter 3 in the *Companion Reader.* Highlight selections from the *Companion Reader* that you feel are particularly helpful for this week's lesson.

- Read the Scripture passages assigned for the week:
  - Day 1: John 15:1-11
  - Day 2: Psalm 122
  - Day 3: Psalm 100; Psalm 29:1-3
  - Day 4: Matthew 26:17-30; Mark 14:12-26; Luke 22:7-20; Acts 2:41-47; 1 Corinthians 11:17-34
  - Day 5: Hebrews 10:19-25; Philippians 3:7-16

- Prepare copies of the following handouts found on the CD-ROM for each member of the class:
  - Small-group Overview (copies were distributed at the end of Session 2; print additional copies for those who were not at Session 2 or who might forget to bring it to class with them)
  - A Money Autobiography (Session 4 folder)

- Have available a copy of *The Book of Common Prayer, The United Methodist Hymnal, The United Methodist Book of Worship*, other hymnals or songbooks that your church uses on a regular basis, and a pew Bible. If desired, you also might choose to have available copies of the United Methodist studies on baptism (*By Water and the Spirit*) and Communion (*This Holy Mystery*) and brochures on baptism and Communion published by Abingdon Press (see p. 14 for a listing of titles).

- Provide copies of the bulletin from a recent worship service at your church. If your church does not use printed bulletins, ask the worship team for a copy of the outline for the most recent worship service(s).

Sign-in / Objectives (2 minutes)

- Invite participants to sign in and make a nametag. If the group is smaller and seated around a table, tent cards are another option for names.

- Share the objectives of the session. Participants will:
  1. Understand the importance of connecting with other Christians through worship and small-group community.
  2. Understand what worship is and what it means to worship in Spirit and truth.

3. Explore different styles of worship and how United Methodists worship.
4. Explore the benefits of small-group community.

Opening Prayer (1 minute)

• Read the following prayer, offer a spontaneous prayer, or invite a participant to pray.

Lord of all creation,
You are here within us, among us, around us.
We come to this time of sharing with joy and hope.
Open our minds to your guidance in prayer
* and study.*
Awaken our hearts to your presence.
As we learn to focus on your love and turn again
* to you,*
All praise and honor is yours, O Lord,
Now and from this day forward. Amen.

Biblical Foundation (2 minutes)

• Read Psalm 100 in unison. Don't worry about participants reading from different translations; it's all part of the "joyful noise"!

• Summary: This psalm is an ancient song of thanksgiving and praise. It reminds us of the joy of true worship and the steadfast goodness of God.

• Suggested talking points:
   ○ A true sense of presence has energy, joy, thanksgiving, and praise!

○ When we focus on God in worship and small groups, we find that God is already there, ready to fill us with grace and love.

Daily Workbook Discussion
(45 minutes for 60-minute session; 55 minutes for 90-minute session)

"Archbishop Desmond Tutu demonstrate[s] the importance of the African concept of *ubuntu*, which he define[s] as meaning, 'My humanity is caught up, is inextricably bound up, in yours. . . . A person is a person through other persons.' We find our humanity in our connections with others. A self-made individual is an oxymoron. I am who I am because you are who you are."[4]
—*Companion Reader,* Chapter 3

Work through the following outline, using the interactive elements as they are presented. Invite class members to refer to the notes, responses, and questions they recorded through the week as the discussion progresses.

Understand the Importance of Connecting with Other Christians Through Worship and Small-group Community

• Ask class members to share their understanding of the Methodist societies, class meetings, and bands (see *Daily Workbook,* page 50). Lead a conversation on how they relate to the discipleship pathway. Suggested talking points:

- Societies relate to our larger community, specifically the gathering for worship and member care. They are a gateway for those new to the faith and a calling for all disciples to regularly focus on God.
- Class meetings focused on learning the faith and the accountability of disciples in a teacher/student model.
- Bands took discipleship deeper and focused on mutual accountability and spiritual growth.
- Why do people attend worship, participate in small groups, belong to a church? Why is it important to do so? (see *Daily Workbook* questions, page 51)

Understand What Worship Is and What It Means to Worship in Spirit and Truth

- Invite class members to share a meaningful experience of worship and why it was important to them. Look for common factors in the responses, such as relationships, closeness to God, personal circumstance, and attitude.

- Read and invite responses to John 4:24: "God is spirit, and those who worship him must worship in spirit and truth" (NRSV).

- Ask class members to share what *presence* means to them (see *Daily Workbook*, page 53) and how it relates to worship.

- Read the definition of *liturgy* from page 54 in the *Daily Workbook*: "Liturgy is a prescribed ritual for public worship and is derived from the Greek *leitourgia*, which means 'work of the people.' "

- Ask what difference it makes to consider worship as "work"—or to consider the worshiper's role as that of an actor rather than an audience member (see below).

> Theologian Søren Kierkegaard once said that many churches have a model of worship in which the people leading worship are the actors, God is the off-stage director, and the congregation is the audience. He offered a better understanding by saying that the people leading worship should be the directors, the congregation should be understood to be the actors, with God as the audience.
> *Daily Workbook*, Week 3, Day 3

- Ask class members:
  - How do you prepare for worship?
  - What do you expect from worship?
  - What are the factors that influence your experience of worship? (See *Daily Workbook* questions on page 53.)

Explore Different Styles of Worship and How United Methodists Worship

- Outline the basic order of worship in UM congregations:
  - **[In]Gathering / entrance:** "We are so easily intoxicated with the values, attitudes, and priorities of the world that we might

as well be asleep to the presence of God. Worship begins by awakening us from the intoxicating stupor of the culture around us. We are called to wake up to what God has done and is doing in Jesus Christ." (*Companion Reader*, page 43)

○ **Proclamation of the Word:** "Whatever forms we use, we tell the story in order to find our place within it so that the story becomes our own." (*Companion Reader*, page 44)

○ **Response to the Word:** "Christian worship is a countercultural gathering in which we declare that the risen Christ has overcome every power that would separate us, every force that would divide us, and every evil that would destroy us. In worship we declare that Jesus Christ is Lord over all." (*Companion Reader*, page 45)

○ **Sending forth:** "As worship concludes, we are sent forth into the world in the confidence of the risen Christ. The church gathered for worship becomes the church scattered for witness and service. Having heard the story of God's love in Christ, we are sent out to make that love real to others." (*Companion Reader*, page 45)

• Distribute bulletins or worship service outlines from your congregation's worship service(s) and discuss how your church employs this order of worship.

• Explore the sacraments of baptism and Communion.

• Invite class members who have been baptized to share stories of their baptism to "remember and be thankful." Be prepared to share your own story.

• Invite class members to share stories of their first time taking Communion or a time it was particularly meaningful. Be prepared to share a story of your own. (See *Daily Workbook*, page 59.)

"There are times when I come to worship to affirm the faith that I hold, but there are other times when I come to worship so that the faith the church affirms can hold me. There are times when I come to sing my song of hope, but there are other times when I need the church to sing that song for me. There are times when I am present with the men in my small group in order to encourage someone else, and there are times when I need to be present so they can encourage me."
—*Companion Reader,* Chapter 3

Explore the Benefits of Small-group Community

• Review the Small-group Community Profile (*Daily Workbook*, page 110).

• Instruct participants to summarize their responses.

• Ask participants to get out their copies of the Small-group Community Overview (distributed at the end of Session 2). Provide additional copies to those who were not present in Session 2 or who forgot to bring the form with them. Ask everyone to complete and turn in the top portion, cutting or tearing along the dotted line. The handout is both a list of small-group options in your church and a response to be collected and shared for follow up with the group or individual(s) charged with connecting members to the life of the church. If your church does not currently have this function, consider suggesting the creation of such a team or ministry to the pastor or Church Council chair for follow up with future courses of *A Disciple's Path*.

- Ask class members to respond to the idea of turning committees into communities (see *Companion Reader,* page 40).

Optional Activity
(20 minutes, 90-minute session only)

- Explore Acts 2:42-47 using *Lectio Divina*.

Looking Ahead to Next Week
(5 minutes)

- Remind participants to pray daily during the week, including for their prayer partners.

- Tell participants that next week's focus is Gifts: Financial Generosity. Instruct them to complete Week 4 in the *Daily Workbook* and read chapter 4 in the *Companion Reader* before the next session. Emphasize that completing the material in the *Daily Workbook* will enrich the next session for everyone.

- Distribute copies of A Money Autobiography (included in the Session 4 folder on the CD-ROM) and instruct participants to complete it in the coming week. This is an exercise for their use

only. They will not be asked to share details but to reflect on the experience and lessons learned from completing the exercise.

- Ask if there are any questions.

Take-home Message and Closing Prayer (5 minutes)

- Have participants stand in a circle.

- Ask each participant to share his or her "take home" message—the one thing that spoke most loudly or clearly from today's session.

- Offer a closing prayer—the one below or a spontaneous prayer of your own. Consider asking for a volunteer to lead opening and closing prayers next week.

Gracious and loving God, we are grateful for your presence among us and within us as we have shared and learned from one another. We ask that you continue to be with each member of this group as we move through the coming week—working, playing, studying, and praying— until we come together again to deepen our understanding of the discipleship path and how to travel it together. Amen.

Session 4
Gifts: Financial Generosity

Preparation

- Complete the reading and questions for Week 4 in the *Daily Workbook* and read chapter 4 in the *Companion Reader*. Highlight selections from the *Companion Reader* that you feel are particularly helpful for this week's lesson.

- Read the Scripture passages assigned for the week:
  - Day 1: Luke 12:14-21; Psalm 24:1-2; Matthew 25:14-30; 1 Timothy 6:17-18; James 1:17; 2 Corinthians 8:9
  - Day 2: Numbers 18:21, 25-31; Deuteronomy 13:22-29; Matthew 6:1-4, 19-21; 23:23; Malachi 3:8-12
  - Day 3: Luke 21:1-4; John 3:16; 1 Corinthians 13:3; 2 Corinthians 8:1-5; 9:1-15
  - Day 4: Matthew 6:2-4; Mark 12:41-44; Luke 12:48; 21:1-4; Acts 20:32-35
  - Day 5: Matthew 6:21; 25:14-30; Proverbs 3:9

- Prepare copies of the following handouts found on the CD-ROM for each member of the class:
  - Money Matters Glossary
  - Plain Rules for Generosity

- If you would like to include video in the session, obtain a copy of Rob Bell's NOOMA "Rich" video. (View a trailer at http://www.youtube.com/watch?v=VZFFxDcSfeA. To order a download or DVD, see http://nooma.com/nooma-rich-013-rob-bell.php.) Make arrangements to have the appropriate equipment for viewing the video, and be sure to test the equipment before class.

- If possible, obtain a copy of your church's most recent budget to illustrate the ways in which the church observes the various forms of tithing.

- Gather information about the benefits derived and ministry accomplished through United Methodist apportionment dollars. Information on apportionments is available online at www.umcgiving.org. Resources may be available from your conference office about regional ministries. You may also obtain copies of *The United Methodist Handbook* or other United Methodist resources that offer information about apportionments.[5]

- If your faith community has a catalog or descriptive listing of ministry opportunities, secure copies for each participant. Or refer participants to information about ministry opportunities on your church website.

Sign-in / Objectives (2 minutes)

- Invite participants to sign in and make a nametag. If the group is smaller and seated around a table, tent cards are another option for names.

- Share the objectives of the session. Participants will:
  - Explore the spiritual discipline of financial generosity.
  - Understand that everything belongs to God and giving is about the heart.
  - Discuss and understand the tithe.
  - Understand the importance of regular and consistent giving.
  - Explore the 10-10-80 principle.
  - Understand the channels of giving in the local United Methodist church and the denomination.
  - Identify next steps for financial giving.

Opening Prayer (1 minute)

- Read the following prayer, offer a spontaneous prayer, or invite a participant to pray.

God of abundance,
Thank you for the riches of love
  you pour into our lives.
As we learn to know you in prayer and study,

As we turn to you in worship and in community,
Teach us to reflect your generosity
  in the way we live our lives
    and support the work of your church. Amen.

Biblical Foundation
(2 minutes)

- Read 1 Timothy 6:17-18.

Note: Read the passage yourself or invite a group member to read it.

- Summary: The author instructs Timothy, who is leading the church in Ephesus, to advise the congregation about their attitude toward "riches." He defines true riches as hope in God, the source of all good things. The people should reflect that sense of abundance in their attitude and behavior through good works, generosity, and sharing.

- Suggested talking points:
  - Our session today will focus on the definition of riches and the ways in which we reflect God's love through our lives of generosity in spirit and in practice.
  - By the end of the session, we hope that you see yourself as rich.

Daily Workbook Discussion
(45 minutes for 60-minute session;
55 minutes for 90-minute session)

Work through the following outline, using the interactive elements as they are presented. Invite the class members to refer to the notes, responses, and questions they recorded through the week as the discussion progresses.

Explore the Spiritual Discipline of Financial Generosity

- Lead a discussion about the Money Autobiography exercise, which you distributed at the end of Session 3. Have extra copies on hand for reference, if desired.
  - What value did participants find in it?
  - What was challenging?
  - What was surprising?
  - What has changed in their relationship with God and money over time? (See also *Daily Workbook* questions on page 68.)

It's All God's and Giving Is About the Heart

- Share the following quotations from the week's readings:
  - "Once we are able to offer God control of our finances, we can offer God our entire lives and experience the spiritual freedom and joy that God intends for us." (*Daily Workbook*, page 66)
  - "God looks at the motivation of your heart and is not impressed or pleased by loveless giving. The only form of sacrificial giving that God does not seem to appreciate is sacrificial giving without love." (*Daily Workbook*, page 72)
  - "Put what, why, and who you love ahead of what, why, and who you don't, and your roadmap will begin to write itself. . . . In our

frantic pursuit of 'more, bigger, faster, cheaper, nastier,' the tragic result is that we end up putting 'what, why, and who we love' at the end of the list. . . . The roadmap we need to follow is one that leads us 'somewhere that matters—not just somewhere that glitters.' "[6] (*Companion Reader*, page 48)

> "No one can serve two masters; for a slave will either hate the one and love the other, or be devoted to the one and despise the other. You cannot serve God and wealth."
> —Matthew 6:24 NRSV

- Distribute copies of Money Matters Glossary (CD-ROM) and ask the class to record their definitions of abundance, enough, generosity, need, ownership, riches, stewardship, and treasure. Invite class members to share their definitions.

Discuss and Understand the Tithe

- As you work through the following material on the three types of tithes offered by the Israelites, invite class members to read the relevant Scripture verses. At the end of each section, pose the question printed in bold type.

1. Every year, the people paid a general tithe for the support of the Levites (Numbers 18:21).

All the tribes of Israel, except the Levites, had a designated geographical area as their inheritance. The Levites—in return for their work within the nation—received income tax of 10 percent from the rest of the population.

The Levites functioned as health inspectors, police, justices, and teachers. To put it simply, the Levites provided the public services for the Israelites, and they were supported by a system of income tax called "tithes."

The Tithe within the Tithe, Numbers 18:25-31: The priests and those who maintained the temple were also Levites, and the Levites paid a tithe of the general tithe to the priests among them. All the priests were Levites, but not all Levites were priests. The priestly caste were descended from Aaron and had specific responsibilities related to temple worship. The tithe of the tithe guaranteed the financial security of the priests, and thereby protected the temple system.

Ask the class to identify the ways we support the work of today's public servants and "priests."

2. Every year, the people put aside a tithe to pay for their annual pilgrimages to Jerusalem (Deuteronomy 14:22-26).

The people of Israel were required to assemble three times a year at Jerusalem (the place chosen by the Lord) for the major feasts. This was meant to be a time of rejoicing, and the Lord ensured that everybody had sufficient resources to fully enter into the celebration by commanding that they set aside 10 percent of their annual income for that purpose.

The next verse (v. 27) includes the reminder, "Do not neglect the Levites." The second tithe for the annual feasts was not to be confused with the separate and distinct general tithe for the Levites and the priests.

Ask the class how it changes their understanding of the tithe to think of it as paying for their celebrations of God's glory.

3. Every third year, the people paid a tithe for the poor, the orphans, and the widows (Deuteronomy 14:28-29).

Social justice and care for the poor and marginalized was always part of God's plan. The third-year tithe was a disciplinary provision for the less-fortunate members of society.

Ask the class to identify the ways in which the church supports the poor and marginalized in today's society.

Understand the Importance of Regular and Consistent Giving

• Point out that "we give back to God what is God's so that through our gifts the love of God can become a tangible reality in our world." (Daily Workbook, page 69)

• Explore Wesley's three rules for dealing with money:

- Gain all you can: without hurting your health, your mind, or your neighbor.
- Save all you can: this is not hoarding, but living *frugally* ("without waste").
- Give all you can: "The purpose of the discipline of generosity is for our lives to be shaped into the likeness of the extravagant generosity of God."

(See *Companion Reader,* pages 49-50.)

Explore the 10-10-80 Principle

- Review the principle:
  - Give the first 10 percent to God.
  - Save the next 10 percent.
  - Live on the remaining 80 percent.

(See *Daily Workbook,* page 76.)

- Show Rob Bell's video NOOMA "Rich." (optional)

- Invite participants to share responses to the 10-10-80 principle. Is it possible or desirable in their lives? What would have to change for them to approach this discipline? What would make it worth the effort? What are the benefits of not living in this way (what is our resistance to change)?

Understand the Channels of Giving in the Local Congregation and in the Denomination

- If you have been able to obtain the church's budget and information about the beneficial use of apportionment dollars in your local congregation, conference, and the denomination, share that information with the class.

- List together the varieties of ways that people give to the church.

Identify Next Steps for Financial Giving

- Review the rules on generous giving (*Companion Reader,* pages 53-54):

  - "Generosity begins with God." We give in loving response to God's gifts to us.
  - "Generosity is essential. Our use of money undergoes a fundamental transformation when we stop asking how much of our wealth we will give to God and start asking how much of God's wealth we will keep for ourselves."
  - "Generosity is intentional." Repeat the 10-10-80 principle.
  - "Generosity grows with practice." As we learn to give, we learn to love giving and want to give more.
  - "Generosity is joyful." When you give a gift chosen with care, it makes you feel wonderful.
  - "Generosity results in blessing." Giving for the sake of giving is reflected in the lives of those who receive and those who give.

- Distribute the handout Plain Rules for Generosity and invite class members to complete it.

Optional Activity (20 minutes, 90-minute session only)

- Using the SOAPY method, explore Matthew 6:19-20: "Do not store up for yourselves treasures on earth, where moth and rust consume and where thieves break in and steal; but store up for yourselves treasures in heaven, where neither moth nor rust consumes and where thieves do not break in and steal" (NRSV).

- If you choose to do this activity, complete it before having class members identify their next steps for financial giving.

Looking Ahead to Next Week (5 minutes)

- Remind participants to pray daily during the week, including for their prayer partners.

- Tell participants that next week's focus is Service: Spiritual Gifts and Gifts-based Service. Instruct them to complete Week 5 in the *Daily Workbook* and read chapter 5 in the *Companion Reader* before the next session. Emphasize that completing the material in the *Daily Workbook* will enrich the next session for everyone.

- Instruct class members to complete the Spiritual Gifts Discovery Tool at http://www.ministrymatters.com/ spiritualgifts/ and complete the Gifts-based Service Profile in the Appendix of the Daily Workbook before the next session.

- Distribute copies of your church's catalog or descriptive listing of ministry opportunities, or instruct participants how to locate this information on the church website. Tell participants they will use this information as part of a reflective activity during the week.

- Ask if there are any questions.

Take-home Message and Closing Prayer (5 minutes)

- Have participants stand in a circle.

- Ask each participant to share his or her "take-home" message—the one thing that spoke most loudly or clearly from today's session.

- Offer a closing prayer—the one below or a spontaneous prayer of your own. Consider asking for a volunteer to lead opening and closing prayers next week.

Gracious and loving God, we are grateful for your presence among us and within us as we have shared and learned from one another. We ask that you continue to be with each member of this group as we move through the coming week—working, playing, studying, and praying—until we come together again to deepen our understanding of the discipleship path and how to travel it together. Amen.

Session 5

Service: Spiritual Gifts and Gifts-based Service

Preparation

- Complete the reading and questions for Week 5 in the *Daily Workbook*, review the Spiritual Gifts Descriptions in the *Daily Workbook* Appendix, and read chapter 5 in the *Companion Reader*. Highlight selections from the Companion Reader that you feel are particularly helpful for this week's lesson.

- Read the Scripture passages assigned for the week:
  - Day 1: 1 Peter 2:4-10; 4:8-11
  - Day 2: Romans 12:4-8; 1 Corinthians 12:1-31; Ephesians 4:1-16
  - Day 3: John 13:14-15; Romans 12:1-6; Ephesians 4:12; James 1:22-25, 27; 2:14-17
  - Day 4: 1 Corinthians 12:18-27
  - Day 5: Exodus 2:11-14; 3:7-8; Matthew 25:34-40; Ephesians 2:10

- Complete your own Spiritual Gifts assessment (http://www.ministrymatters.com/spiritualgifts/).

- Prepare copies of the following handouts found on the CD-ROM for each member of the class:
  - Gifted in Community
  - Gifts-based Service Profile

  - Spiritual Gifts Bingo (if you are doing the optional activity; prepare at least one copy of each of the five "bingo" handouts for use by teams or individuals)
  - Commitment Card (pages 1 and 2). Use the Commitment Card on the CD-ROM as a sample for creating your own, or if you have access to Adobe Illustrator 5.1, modify the file and print copies on the desired paper size and stock (front and back). Distribute the cards at the end of Session 5. (Participants will complete them during the week and bring them to the last session.)

- In advance, invite three or four church leaders who serve in diverse areas of ministry to attend the session. Ask them to share a story or prepare a statement about the ways they live out of their spiritual gifts. The story or statement should be brief, about 3-5 minutes. If you need help identifying appropriate persons to invite, ask the pastor for help. (If desired, you may choose to invite one or more of these individuals to serve as mentors or conversation partners before, during, or immediately following Session 6.)

- In preparation for completing a Commitment Card, participants will have an opportunity to be in conversation with a mentor or conversation partner who can help to guide them in their next steps in gifts-based service in the congregation and beyond. You may approach this task any way that suits your needs. Here are three possibilities:
  1) Invite someone to speak to the entire group during Session 6 (be sure to include time for questions, answers, and discussion).
  2) Invite a team of persons to meet individually or in small groups with participants during Session 6. This may be a team designated by your church to fill this role or persons you identify and invite. Make sure enough rooms are available for the conversations to afford privacy.
  3) Invite a team of persons to meet with individuals or in small groups with participants outside of class time. Ideally, this should take place prior to Session 6, if at all possible, or soon thereafter. Create a schedule of times when conversation partners are available to meet and have each participant sign up for a time during Session 5. Follow up to be sure all meetings occurred as planned.
     - If having these conversations *before* Session 6, instruct participants to take their Commitment Cards with them to review and discuss with their conversation partners and then bring the cards to the last session. After collecting the cards in the session, give them to the appropriate individual(s) for follow up.
     - If having these conversations *after* Session 6, instruct participants to bring their Commitment Cards to the last session. After collecting the cards in the session, distribute them to the appropriate conversation partners in advance of the scheduled meetings for discussion and follow up.

Sign-in / Objectives (2 minutes)

- Invite participants to sign in and make a name tag. If the group is smaller and seated around a table, tent cards are another option for names.

- Share the objectives of the session. Participants will:
  - Learn about the nature and value of spiritual gifts.
  - Explore servanthood (servant vs. volunteer).
  - Name and celebrate one another's spiritual gifts.
  - Identify a holy discontent and how to use spiritual gifts.
  - Discern the next step in the journey of gifts-based service.
  - Offer insights on areas of interest and desired connection in ministry.

Opening Prayer (1 minute)

- Read the following prayer, offer a spontaneous prayer, or invite a participant to pray.

O Holy Spirit, you fill us with the breath of life,
  the power of grace.
Help us to be aware of your presence
  within us and among us,

That we may open our hearts and minds
   to understand these gifts you give,
   to use them together in your service,
   to know and to do your will.
In the name of Jesus the Christ, we pray. Amen.

Biblical Foundation (2 minutes)

• Read 1 Peter 2:4-10.

Note: *Read the passage yourself or invite a group member to read it.*

• Provide a brief summary of the passage. Example: The author of 1 Peter invites us as disciples to become like Christ, "living stones" to be built into God's house. As a royal priesthood, we are set apart, not for privilege but to proclaim the love of God to all the world.

• Suggested talking points:
   ○ In the royal priesthood of all believers, no one person is more important than any other, and none of us can build the house of God alone. All are valuable and critical to the work of glorifying God and learning to share the good news. Our salvation is individual and communal.
   ○ *The Book of Discipline of The United Methodist Church* states the following: "All Christians are called through their baptism to this ministry of servanthood in the world to the glory of God and for human fulfillment."[7]

Daily Workbook Discussion
(45 minutes for 60-minute session;
55 minutes for 90-minute session)

Work through the following outline, using the interactive elements as they are presented. Invite the class members to refer to the notes, responses, and questions they recorded through the week as the discussion progresses.

Learn About the Nature and Value of Spiritual Gifts

• Lead a brief discussion on what participants learned about spiritual gifts from their reading this week.

• Spiritual gifts are:
   ○ expressions of God's grace.
   ○ the power of the Holy Spirit— breath or fire—like the *ruach* (Hebrew) that breathed life into the first earth creature and the *pneuma* (Greek) that filled the first believers at Pentecost with boldness to share the good news.
   ○ innate in each and every person, waiting to be released and shared equally valuable.

> "God's idea of a good time is to accomplish God's saving purpose in this world through ordinary people . . . who discover their gifts and release them for God's work in the world. The challenge for every follower of Christ is to use the gift that God has given, trusting that God will use it in ways beyond our imagination."
> —*Companion Reader*, Chapter 5

- given for the common good, for building up the body of Christ—the church—for the transformation of the world into God's kingdom.
- powers given to equip us to do the work to which God calls us in this time and place.
- truly powerful when joined in community.
- a source of joy in discovery and blessing when shared with others.
- lived out within the church and in our daily lives.

• Spiritual gifts are not:
- natural abilities and talents, although we may live out our gifts using our natural abilities and talents.
- skills, roles, and functions of ministry and life, although God uses our gifts to bring life and energy to all of these.
- given so we can boast or feel superior to anyone else inside or beyond the church.

• Review the stories in the *Companion Reader* (chapter 5, pages 59-60) that offer three significant perspectives on living out our gifts: the joy of saying yes to God's call at the right time and

> "If we want to experience the life that God intends for us, there comes a point where we shift from being merely recipients of grace to being channels of grace to others. . . .We no longer hold God's love for ourselves but find ways to share it with others. . . . We stop being spectators and become participants in God's transformation of the world."
> —*Companion Reader*, Chapter 5

place; living into the meaning and power of our gifts, even when we don't quite understand them; and embracing the freedom to say no appropriately when the call of our gifts is clear.

Explore Servanthood (Servant vs. Volunteer)

• Point out that "the word *volunteer* means different things to different people, but it is not a word we find in the Bible. The New Testament word is *servant*" (*Daily Workbook*, page 85). Make two columns on newsprint or a whiteboard, labeling them "volunteer" and "servant." Identify the differences between a volunteer and a servant, and record participants' responses.

> "I have often likened congregational life to breathing. . . . Sustainable health depends on balance—inhaling (inward practices that develop us in our faith and abilities to serve) and exhaling (applying what we learn in service to others)." [8]
> —Dan R. Dick

Example

Volunteer	Servant
choice	calling
your schedule	your life
adds value	guiding value
human venture	God's action
acting on desire	hearing and doing God's will

• Take a moment to focus on and offer insights about the idea of balance in our life of servanthood. We need to both hear and do (see *Daily Workbook,* pages 85-86).

> "When we talk about passion in the context of spiritual gifts, we mean . . . a God-given desire to help in healing a broken world. The prophet Jeremiah described it as 'a burning fire shut up in my bones' (Jeremiah 20:9 NRSV). He was weary holding it in, but he could hold it no longer."
> —*Daily Workbook*, Week 5, Day 5

• Some class members may share a concern that servanthood sounds like being a "doormat." Share with the class the difference between *humility* and *humiliation*:

- *humility*—the joy of giving control to God; willingly putting oneself aside for the sake of another; recognizing the learning potential in each positive and negative experience; a positive attitude. The humble person gives to others without ever losing a sense of self.
- *humiliation*—experiencing loss or defeat as shame; giving control of one's responses to others; a negative attitude. The humiliated person allows the judgments of others to define the sense of self.

Name and Celebrate One Another's Spiritual Gifts

• Distribute the handout Gifted in Community (CD-ROM) and talk briefly about the fact that the lists vary. Just as each person is uniquely gifted, so each community of faith is uniquely gifted by God to fill the needs of a specific time and place. While some gifts appear on each list, none is more important or valuable than another (see 1 Corinthians 12:14-26).

• Invite participants to share their top gifts identified by the spiritual gifts discovery tool. Celebrate the unique collection of God's power at work in just this one room!

Identify a Holy Discontent and How to Use Spiritual Gifts

• Ask for responses to the questions related to holy discontent (*Daily Workbook*, pages 91-92).

• Note that Frederick Buechner reminds us that God's will resides where our deep passion and the world's deep hunger meet.[9]

Discern the Next Step in the Journey of Gifts-based Service

• Point out that discernment is the prayerful act of listening for God's will. Invite the participants to rest their brains and open their inner ear to hear God speak through the Word.

• Explore Romans 12:2 together using *Lectio Divina:* "Do not be conformed to this world, but be transformed by the renewing of your minds, that you may discern what is the will of God—what is good and acceptable and perfect" (NRSV).

- Talking points:
  - "You" in this verse is plural. This is a call to the entire community.
  - The Greek word translated here as "minds" means much more than the brain; it encompasses the entire self—heart, soul, body, mind, and spirit.
  - As the body of Christ, we are set apart ("do not be conformed to this world") as individuals and as a community, called to discipleship ("be transformed by the renewing of your minds"), and sent to fulfill God's will ("what is good and acceptable and perfect").

Offer Insights on Areas of Interest and Desired Connection in Ministry

- Distribute the Gifts-based Service Profile and instruct participants to complete this form based on their notes and reflections in the *Daily Workbook*. Participants should have completed the Gifts-based Service Profile found in the Appendix, and they may simply copy their responses. Explain that the intent is for them to have a copy to keep and a copy to turn in. Collect the completed profiles and use them to guide you in choosing guests to serve as mentors or conversation partners for Session 6 (unless you plan to use the same guests for both Session 5 and Session 6). Give the profiles to the invited conversation partners to use as conversation guides (prior to, during, or after Session 6).

- Welcome the church leaders that you invited to come and share a story or statement about the ways they live out of their spiritual gifts. Invite

class members to listen to their stories of ministry.

Optional Activity
(20 minutes, 90-minute session only)

- Extend your time with the invited guests, allowing them to share more about servanthood and the use of spiritual gifts in the service of building up the body of Christ.

- If your guests cannot stay or you prefer to do an activity, play Spiritual Gifts Bingo. Divide the group into five teams. Distribute a Spiritual Gifts Bingo handout (CD-ROM) to each team. Give the teams up to 10 minutes to fill in the sheets, selecting biblical characters that you believe possessed that gift. Tell participants to be sure they can explain why the character fits the gift. All twenty gifts included in the online spiritual gifts discovery tool and the Spiritual Gifts Descriptions (*Daily Workbook* Appendix) are included on the sheets. After the first group is done, allow the other groups to complete their sheets. In the time remaining, invite teams to share their answers and their reasons. This peer learning exercise will deepen the group's understanding of the spiritual gifts.

Looking Ahead to Next Week
(5 minutes)

- Remind participants to pray daily during the week, including for their prayer partners.

- Tell participants that next week's focus is Witness: Invitational Evangelism. Instruct them to complete Week 6 in the *Daily Workbook* and read chapter 6 in the *Companion Reader* before the next session. Emphasize that completing the material in the *Daily Workbook* will enrich the next session for everyone.

- Remind the class that the next session is your final session together. In addition to learning about the practice of witness, you also will be recording the next steps each person will commit to make in his or her journey on the discipleship pathway.

- Tell participants that one or more guests will be coming to the last session to serve as "conversation partners." They will talk one-on-one with participants about how they may serve in ministry both within and beyond the church and will answer any questions they may have as they complete their commitment cards. Or, if you choose to have these mentoring conversations at scheduled times outside of class, provide a schedule of times when conversation partners will be available to meet with participants and have participants sign up for those conversations now. (*Ideally* participants should have the opportunity to have these conversations prior to Session 6. If that is not feasible, schedule the conversations as soon after Session 6 as possible.)

- Consider celebrating the completion of *A Disciple's Path* with a shared meal after your last session—or at some other scheduled time. Talk with participants about this and make plans.

- Ask if there are any questions.

Take-home Message and Closing Prayer (5 minutes)

- Have participants stand in a circle.

- Ask each participant to share his or her "take-home" message—the one thing that spoke most loudly or clearly from today's session.

- Offer a closing prayer—the one below or a spontaneous prayer of your own. Consider asking for a volunteer to lead opening and closing prayers next week.

Gracious and loving God, we are grateful for your presence among us and within us as we have shared and learned from one another. We ask that you continue to be with each member of this group as we move through the coming week—working, playing, studying, and praying— until we come together again to deepen our understanding of the discipleship path and how to travel it together. Amen.

SESSION 6
WITNESS: INVITATIONAL EVANGELISM

Preparation

- Complete the reading and questions for Week 6 in the *Daily Workbook* and read chapter 6 in the *Companion Reader*. Highlight selections from the *Companion Reader* that you feel are particularly helpful for this week's lesson.

- Read the Scripture passages assigned for the week:
  - Day 1: Romans 5:1-21; Acts 3:11-26
  - Day 2: John 2:35-51
  - Day 3: Romans 10:13-17
  - Day 4: 2 Corinthians 10:1-5; 2 Timothy 4:1-2; 1 John 1:1-3; Matthew 5:14-16
  - Day 5: Matthew 28:16-28; Acts 1:1-8
  - A Final Day: 1 Timothy 4:7-8; Luke 9:23-27

- Prepare copies of the following handouts found on the CD-ROM for each member of the class:
  - John Wesley's Covenant Prayer
  - Evaluation Form
  - Extra Commitment Cards for those who forget to bring theirs to class (Session 5 folder)

- Review your options related to involving conversation partners and completing Commitment Cards and prepare accordingly:

1) Invite someone to speak to the entire group during this final session (be sure to include time for questions, answers, and discussion).

2) Invite a team of persons to meet individually or in small groups with participants during this session. This may be a team designated by your church to fill this role or persons you identify and invite. (If desired, these may be the same persons who shared their stories during Session 5.) Make sure enough rooms are available for the conversations to afford privacy.

3) Invite a team of persons to meet individually or in small groups with participants *outside of class time.* Ideally, this should take place prior to this final session, if possible, or soon thereafter. If choosing this option and participants have not met with their conversation partners prior to Session 6, provide a schedule of times when conversation partners will be available to meet and have each participant sign up for a time. Follow up to be sure all meetings occurred as planned.

- If having these conversations *before* Session 6, participants should take their Commitment Cards with them to review and discuss with their conversation partners and then bring the cards to the last session. After collecting the cards in the session, give them to the appropriate individual(s) for follow up.
- If having these conversations *after* Session 6, have participants bring their commitment cards to the last session. After collecting the cards in the session, distribute them to the appropriate conversation partners in advance of the scheduled meetings for discussion and follow up.

- If you plan to use the suggested ritual for collecting Commitment Cards (see page 59), arrange to have someone lead the singing and provide a suitable basket or decorated box to receive the cards.

- If you are having a 90-minute session and choose to do the Optional Activity, obtain a copy of Rob Bell's NOOMA "Bullhorn Guy" video. (View a trailer at http://www.youtube.com/watch?v=EsIfntfLYPI&feature=related. To order a download or DVD, see http://store.flannel.org/films/nooma/009.html.) Make arrangements to have the appropriate equipment for viewing the video, and be sure to test the equipment before class.

- If you plan to extend the session time for a celebration, make arrangements for food, servers, and room set up and clean up. If you are having a guest or a team of individuals hold conversations with participants during this session, consider inviting them to join in the celebratory meal.

- Arrange for any additional paperwork to be completed by participants who will be joining the congregation as new members.

Sign-in /Objectives (2 minutes)

- Invite participants to sign in and make a nametag. If the group is smaller and seated around a table, tent cards are another option for names.

- Share the objectives of the session. Participants will:
  - Understand what invitational evangelism is.
  - Identify their own evangelism style.
  - Review membership vows and make a decision about membership (for those in a membership class).
  - Complete a Commitment Card.

Opening Prayer (1 minute)

- Read the following prayer, offer a spontaneous prayer, or invite a participant to pray.

Gracious and loving God,
You have filled us to overflowing with blessings:
the peace of knowing you through prayer and study,
the privilege of your presence in worship
 and in the company of other disciples,

*the joy of reflecting your love in our giving,
the power to share the gifts you give
   in building up the body of Christ.
Send us out now to shine as the light of your grace
   so that all the world may be transformed by your
     love. Amen.*

Biblical Foundation (2 minutes)

- Read John 1:35-49.

Note: Read the passage yourself or invite a group member to read it.

- Summary: This is the call of the disciples, according to the Gospel of John.

- Suggested talking points:
  - Jesus asks Andrew and another of John the Baptist's disciples what they are looking for and calls them to "Come and see."
  - Andrew invites his brother, Simon (Peter), telling him they have found the Messiah.
  - Jesus simply says to Philip, "Follow me."
  - Philip invites Nathanael to "Come and see."
  - No pressure, just simple invitations to new life: Follow me. Come and see. That's invitational evangelism.

Daily Workbook Discussion
(45 minutes for 60-minute session;
55 minutes for 90-minute session)

Work through the following outline, using the interactive elements as they are presented. Invite the class members to refer to the notes, responses, and questions they recorded through the week as the discussion progresses.

Understand What Invitational Evangelism Is

- Share the following excerpt from Chapter 6 in the *Companion Reader:*

  Evangelism comes from the root word meaning "good news." An evangelist is simply a person who shares good news.
  - When was the last time you had some good news to share?
  - When did you see a movie or read a book you enjoyed so much that you couldn't wait to tell someone about it?
  - When did you have a great meal at a new restaurant, and you couldn't wait to take a friend there to experience it?
  - When did you experience love so deep or joy so great that your first response was to invite someone else to experience it?

- Share what invitational evangelism is and is not.

Invitational evangelism is:
- relational; a personal witness
- sharing our story when we are invited to do so
- listening to other people's stories; creating conversations
- an invitation to join the body of Christ

- Invitational evangelism is not:
  - forcing people to hear our stories
  - converting people; only the Holy Spirit can do that
  - keeping people from hell; fear is not very inviting

- Remind the class of the difference between *humility* and *humiliation* (see Session 5, page 49). Invitational evangelism is based in humility and confidence in the good news, never in attempts to humiliate or shame another.

- Ask how the previous statements about evangelism compare with participants' exposure to evangelism in the culture. What is the role of disciples and the community of faith in counteracting negative stereotypes and practices of evangelism?

- Ask for responses to John Wesley's three essential beliefs: original sin, justification by faith, and holiness of heart and mind (*Daily Workbook*, page 94).

Identify Their Own Evangelism Style

- Invite participants to share their response about how experiencing Christ has affected their lives (see *Daily Workbook,* page 100).

- Invite participants to share summaries of their stories of coming to be a follower of Jesus (see *Daily Workbook*, page 103).

- Ask participants if they identified an evangelism style or form of witness that is right for them and why (see *Daily Workbook*, pages 101-02).
  - Intellectual
  - Confrontational
  - Testimonial
  - Interpersonal
  - Invitational
  - Serving

- Review the following guidelines for invitational evangelism from the *Companion Reader* (page 70):
  - **Begin with friendship.** No one wants to be manipulated. Evangelism that is centered in Christlike love for others begins in honest, nonmanipulative, life-giving human friendships. The challenge for many church folks is that all of our friends are already followers of Christ. How many friendships do you have with people who do not yet know Christ?
  - **Listen. Listen. Listen.** It's easy to begin with the assumption that witnessing is all about telling someone about Christ. But Jesus' relationship with Andrew began with a question: "What are you looking for?" (John 1:38). In his conversation with the Samaritan woman at the well, Jesus listened deeply to the thirst in her soul (John 4:1-30). Are you more interested in listening to another's person's story than in sharing your own?

○ **Know your story.** The role of witnesses is not to argue the case or to judge the outcome but simply to tell what they heard, saw, and experienced. Whenever the opportunity came, the apostles were ready to tell the story of the way they met Christ and the difference he had made in their lives. Can you tell the story of your relationship with Christ in a simple, clear, and concise way?

○ **Offer the invitation.** The invitation to "come and see" can take whatever form is appropriate to the situation. It may be a direct invitation to make a commitment to Christ. It may be an invitation to visit your church, to join a small group, or to participate in some form of mission or ministry. It is always an open-ended invitation that begins a journey toward a Christ-centered life.

○ **Trust the Spirit.** Because we believe in prevenient grace, we believe that the love of God is already at work in people's lives before they are even aware of it. They may be more ready than you realize. We can trust the Spirit to prepare the way, to be at work in the relationship, to open the right conversation at the right time, and to give us the right way to respond.

• If you are having a 90-minute session and are not including a speaker or conversation partners during class time, you may choose to show Rob Bell's video NOOMA "Bullhorn Guy" now (see Optional Activity).

> "Anyone can try to be a follower of Christ, but the only people who actually discover the life to which God has called us are those who train for it."[10]
> —John Ortberg

Review Membership Vows and Make a Decision About Membership
(for those in a membership class)

• Review the membership vows as we have studied them during *A Disciple's Path:*
  ○ *Prayers:* Prayer and Scripture meditation. What commitment will you make to daily prayer, Bible reflection, and the discipleship pathway?
  ○ *Presence:* Corporate worship and small-group community. How many Sundays each year will you attend worship, fully focused on God? In what small groups will you grow your faith?
  ○ *Gifts:* Financial generosity. How will you reflect the riches of God's grace through your financial commitment to the ministry of the church?
  ○ *Service:* Spiritual gifts and gifts-based service. Where you will follow God's call to serve in the body of Christ?
  ○ *Witness:* Invitational evangelism. How you will listen to the stories of

others, share your faith story, and invite people to the joy of God's love through Jesus Christ and the power of the Holy Spirit?

- Offer a summary statement based on the following excerpt from the Postscript in the *Companion Reader:*

> Through the consistent practice of these spiritual disciplines, the lives of the early Methodists were transformed, and they became a part of God's transformation of the world.
>
> Now the invitation comes to us from the risen Christ, "Follow me!" As disciples of Jesus Christ in The United Methodist Church, we have the challenge to take our next appropriate step along the path that will lead in the direction of a life that is centering in loving God and loving others. How will we respond?

Complete a Commitment Card

Three options have been suggested for giving participants the opportunity to be in conversation with a mentor or conversation partner prior to completing a Commitment Card. Follow the instructions for the option you have chosen.

1) If you invited someone to speak to the entire group during this session:

- Offer a welcome and brief explanation of why he or she is here.
- Pass out copies of John Wesley's Covenant Prayer handout (CD-ROM) and say it aloud together.
- Invite the guest to speak to the group about finding a place to serve within and beyond the congregation according to their giftedness. Encourage participants to ask questions and engage in discussion.
- Ask participants to take out the Commitment Cards they completed during the week. Hand out new cards to those who forgot to bring theirs, and ask them to fill them out now. Allow time for questions and answers at this time.
- Collect the cards. Because rituals help us to remember, consider singing a simple hymn that doesn't require accompaniment, such as "Seek Ye First" (*United Methodist Hymnal* #405) or "Lord, I Want to Be a Christian" (*United Methodist Hymnal* #402) as participants come forward to place their Commitment Cards in a basket or box. As they do so, offer a sign of welcome and validation, such as a handshake, a hug (if that is acceptable), or anointing the forehead with oil in the sign of the cross.
- Be sure to give the cards to the appropriate individual(s) after class for follow up.

2) If you invited a team of persons to meet with individuals or small groups during this session:

- Offer a welcome and brief explanation of why they are here.
- Pass out copies of John Wesley's Covenant Prayer handout (CD-ROM) and say it aloud together.
- Pair or group participants with their conversation partners and invite them to move to the appropriate rooms. Ask them to return in 30 minutes. Participants should take the Commitment Cards they completed during the week with them; hand out new cards to those who forgot to bring theirs to class, and have them complete them with their conversation partners.
- When all participants have returned, collect the cards. Because rituals help us to remember, consider singing a simple hymn that doesn't require accompaniment, such as "Seek Ye First" (*United Methodist Hymnal* #405) or "Lord, I Want to Be a Christian" (*United Methodist Hymnal* #402) as participants come forward to place their Commitment Cards in a basket or box. As they do so, offer a sign of welcome and validation, such as a handshake, a hug (if that is acceptable), or anointing the forehead with oil in the sign of the cross.
  Be sure to give the cards to the appropriate individual(s) after class for follow up.

3) If you invited a team of persons to meet with individuals or small groups *outside of class time*:

- Pass out copies of John Wesley's Covenant Prayer handout (CD-ROM) and say it aloud together.
- Ask participants to get out the Commitment Cards they completed during the week. Hand out new cards to those who forgot to bring theirs, and have them complete them now.
- If participants met with conversation partners *before* this session, ask how those conversations helped to provide guidance or insight, and allow brief discussion.
- If participants plan to meet with conversation partners *after* this session, ask what questions they have for their conversation partners, and allow brief discussion. Be sure everyone has signed up for a time to meet with a conversation partner. Tell participants that their conversation partners will have their Commitment Cards if they should decide they want to make any changes at that time.
- Collect the cards. Because rituals help us to remember, consider singing a simple hymn that doesn't require accompaniment, such as "Seek Ye First" (*United Methodist Hymnal* #405) or "Lord, I Want to Be a Christian" (*United Methodist Hymnal* #402) as participants come forward to

place their Commitment Cards in a basket or box. As they do so, offer a sign of welcome and validation, such as a handshake, a hug (if that is acceptable), or anointing the forehead with oil in the sign of the cross.

- After collecting the cards in the session, distribute them to the appropriate conversation partners in advance of the scheduled meetings for discussion and follow up. Follow up to be sure all conversations have taken place as scheduled.

Optional Activity
(20 minutes, 90-minute session only)

- If you are not having a speaker or conversation partners during class time, you may choose to show Rob Bell's video NOOMA "Bullhorn Guy" *before* reviewing membership vows and completing Commitment Cards. (See p. 57.)

Looking Ahead and Closing Prayer
(10 minutes)

- Hand out copies of the Evaluation Form (CD-ROM) and ask participants to complete them outside of class and return them to you or the church office.

- Have everyone (participants and guests) stand in a circle.

- Invite everyone to commit to continue:
  - praying for class members and listening to God's leading in prayer.

- reading and reflecting on the Bible.
- deepening their awareness of the presence of God in worship and in small-groups.
- working to grow a spirit of generosity, reflected in giving to and through the church.
- learning more about their spiritual gifts and the ways God calls us to live them out in the church and the world.
- sharing the joy of the good news and the abundance of God's grace with those they know and those they meet.

- Ask each group member to share his or her "take home" message—the one thing that spoke most loudly or clearly from today's session or from the entire study.

- Offer a closing prayer—the one below or a spontaneous prayer of your own.

Gracious and loving God, we are grateful for your presence among us and within us as we have shared and learned from one another. We ask that you continue to be with each member of this group as we continue our ongoing journey to deepen our understanding of the discipleship pathway and how to travel it together. Amen.

Celebration

If you have planned a class celebration, move to that time together now.

USING *A DISCIPLE'S PATH* IN A CHURCH-WIDE DISCIPLESHIP INITIATIVE

A Disciple's Path can be used as a church-wide initiative to focus the entire congregation on the life of discipleship. The objective of such a program is to move the congregation to a deeper, more vibrant life in Christ. Following the church-wide initiative, the resources can be used with future new member classes as part of an ongoing discipleship training ministry.

Steps for Planning a Church-wide Initiative
1. Present the idea and resources to leadership and approve dates (six to eight months prior to launch).
2. Form a leadership team to plan and implement the initiative. (Assign at least one staff person to the team—pastor, discipleship staff.)
3. Identify, invite, and train teams (or utilize existing groups) to implement the emphasis—e.g., a communications team, worship team, small-groups team, etc. (See the team role descriptions that follow.)
4. Coordinate with the various teams/groups to create a master timeline and checklist of all tasks.
5. Meet with all adult Sunday school and small-group leaders ahead of the initiative to get buy in and support.
6. Implement the initiative (six week duration).
7. Create a process and system for congregational commitment, assimilation, and training (to ensure that all participating members of the congregation are connected with the ministry of the church through some kind of gifts-based service and are taking next steps in the other areas commitment).

Helpful Ideas
- Have a pilot group complete the study prior to launching the church-wide initiative. Ask participants from the pilot group to share testimonies in worship, small groups, printed materials, videos, and online (both video and print).
- Create events on the Sunday mornings during the initiative that will attract attention and build energy and excitement—such as a ministry fair, leadership dinner, ice cream social, tailgate party, and so forth. HAVE FUN!
- Sell or give away promotional items such as bookmarks, window clings, key tags, and wristbands (available separately; one of each item is included in the *A Disciple's Path* Kit). Here are some ideas for using the items to reinforce key themes of the program:
  o Invite the congregation to wear wristbands on Kick-off Sunday or Commitment Sunday or throughout the entire emphasis. For an ongoing new member program, distribute wristbands during a pastor's coffee or prior to a joining ceremony.

- o Make bookmarks available at the beginning of the study to help participants keep their place in the *Daily Workbook* or *Companion Reader* and to serve as a visual reminder of the definition of a disciple.
- o Distribute window clings during Week 2 on prayer. Encourage participants to put the window cling on a mirror, car windshield, computer screen, or other highly visible place and to read the Wesley covenant prayer daily. Or provide them at the conclusion of the study as part of the commitment ceremony during Session 6.
- o Offer key tags at the beginning or end of the study. Talk about how they may serve as a daily reminder that traveling the discipleship pathway is an ongoing, lifelong journey.
- • Invite leaders of your children's and youth ministries to engage the children and youth in topics that mirror the adult worship themes.
- • Engage children in activities such as a children's poster contest.
- • Plan other events related to the theme or focus of specific weeks. Here are a couple of ideas:
  - o Hold a twenty-four-hour prayer vigil event a few days before the final Sunday, which is Commitment Sunday.
  - o Schedule a church-wide serving day at a local mission during service week.

Six-Week Overview

Week 1: A Disciple's Path Defined
- • Sermon theme: What it means to be a follower of Jesus Christ
- • Key Scripture passage: Luke 10:25-28
- • Take-away: A disciple is a follower of Jesus Christ whose life is centering on loving God and loving others
- • Worship: Program leader or pastor describes the program; recognize leadership team if desired; hymns on discipleship
- • Sunday school classes/small groups: Study Week 1: A Disciple's Path Defined (Note: Classes will need books a week in advance of the group session so that participants may complete the readings and workbook activities for Week 1 prior to the session.)

Week 2: Prayers (Prayer and Scripture Meditation)
- • Sermon theme: Daily prayer rooted in reflection on Scripture
- • Key Scripture passage: Matthew 6:5-15
- • Take-away: Prayer is about cultivating a relationship with God
- • Worship: Emphasis on prayer; hymns on prayer
- • Sunday school classes/small groups: Study Week 2: Prayers

Week 3: Presence (Corporate Worship and Small-group Community)
- • Sermon theme: Christian community in worship, study, and fellowship
- • Key Scripture passage: Psalm 100 (joy of true worship)
- • Take-away: There is no such thing as solitary religion

- Worship: Affirm that we all belong to one another; hymns on Christian community and worship
- Sunday school classes/small groups: Study Week 3: Presence

Week 4: Gifts (Financial Generosity)
- Sermon theme: The spiritual discipline of financial generosity
- Key Scripture passage: 1 Timothy 6:17-18
- Take-away: We give because Jesus gave (Titus 2:14)
- Worship: Emphasis on gratitude; hymns of thanksgiving
- Sunday school classes/small groups: Study Week 4: Gifts

Week 5: Service (Spiritual Gifts and Gifts-based Service)
- Sermon theme: Servanthood
- Key Scripture passage: 1 Peter 2:4-10
- Take-away: Every disciple is called, gifted, and needed in the ministry of the church
- Worship: Emphasis on priesthood of all believers; hymns on servanthood
- Sunday school classes/small groups study Week 5: Service

Week 6: Witness (Invitational Evangelism)
- Sermon theme: Sharing the good news of what God has done in Christ
- Key Scripture passage: John 1:35-49 (Jesus models invitational evangelism)
- Take-away: God can and will use your story if you are ready to share it
- Worship: Emphasis on our role in God's transformation of the world; hymns on the gospel/sharing the gospel
- Sunday school classes/small groups: Study Week 6: Witness

Team Role Descriptions

Communications Team
- Develop the strategy for promoting the initiative. Plan promotional ideas around a logo for posters, banners, and mailings (including e-mail).
- Create and implement a plan for communicating information throughout the initiative. Align weekly e-mail messages from the pastor with each Sunday's theme.
- Draft/edit/design all printed components.
- Work with the church staff to develop a schedule for all printed components and coordinate mailings, newsletter text, and bulletin inserts.
- Hang posters and distribute materials for the program.
- Communicate with staff responsible for website regarding online elements.
- Develop graphics as appropriate.
- Establish print quantities and secure printings.
- Be a participant in one of the small groups.

Small-groups Team
- Work with the adult education department for Sunday school/small-group studies.
- Invite Sunday school/small-group leaders to lead, participate in, and facilitate a six-week class on *A Disciple's Path.*
- Heavily promote the study for full congregational participation.
- Develop training for leaders.
- Be a participant in one of the small groups.

Conversation Partners/Connecting Ministry Team
- Work with the connectional/equipping ministry director to develop a catalog of ministry opportunities and a Commitment Card (see the sample provided on the CD-ROM).
- Serve as conversation partners who meet with small groups or individuals to discuss ministry opportunities for gifts-based service.
- Develop a method for collecting Commitment Cards and recording the responses.
- Communicate the responses to staff and team leaders for follow-up.
- Ensure staff and team leaders have training and assimilation procedures.
- Work with church staff to obtain lists of individuals who have not returned Commitment Cards.
- Ensure follow-up letters are sent out.
- Invite team to make personal contacts of individuals who have not turned in commitments.
- Be a participant in one of the small groups.

Prayer Team
- Recruit participants for continual prayer throughout the six-week initiative.
- Coordinate a prayer vigil to commence twenty-four hours prior to Commitment Sunday and/or the beginning of the study.
- Orchestrate encouragement to leadership team.
- Be a participant in one of the small groups.

Hospitality and Events Team
- Work with the prayer team to make arrangements for a rally or prayer dinner prior to Commitment Sunday or at the beginning of the study.
- Work with various ministries of the church (adult education, congregational care, missions and outreach, connecting/equipping ministry, etc.) to orchestrate special events that highlight different areas inside and outside the church.
- Plan any special events desired to attract and build energy and excitement on the Sundays during the initiative, such as a ministry fair, leadership dinner, ice cream social, tailgate party, etc.

A Disciple's Path Resources Team
- Develop a sales/distribution plan for the book resources and ancillary products.
- Help determine how expenses/money will be handled.
- Be a participant in one of the small groups.

CD-ROM Contents

E-mails

All e-mails are to be sent prior to the session indicated.

Introductory Session
Session1 Option 1
Sesison1 Option 2
Session 2
Session 3
Session 4
Session 5
Session 6

Handouts
(Samples provided on the following pages.)

Introductory Session or Pastor's Coffee
A Disciple's Path Class Covenant
Church History Tree
Introduction to the UMC
Mission, Values, Strategy, Vision
Next-Step Card
Personal Information Form
UM Church History Flowchart
UMC Structure and Organization
What Church Membership Means

Session 1
Mind Mapping Guidelines

Session 2
Who Said That? A Bible Quiz
Who Said That? A Bible Quiz Answer Key

Session 3
Small-group Overview

Session 4
A Money Autobiography
Money Matters Glossary
Plain Rules for Generosity

Session 5
Commitment Card Page 1
Commitment Card Page 2
Gifted in Community
Gifts-based Service Profile
Spiritual Gifts Bingo

Session 6
Evaluation Form
Wesley Covenant Prayer

Sign-in Sheets
Group Session Sign-in Sheet
Pastor's Coffee Sign-in Sheet

PowerPoint Presentations

Introductory Session PowerPoint
Session 1 PowerPoint

A DISCIPLE'S PATH CLASS COVENANT

A Disciple's Path is a study that focuses on what it means to follow Jesus Christ in the path of discipleship, with a special emphasis on what this means to us as followers in the Methodist tradition.

Class Objectives
As a participant in this study, my goals are to:

- learn the discipleship pathway and how to grow my faith in this congregation.
- experience the daily rhythm of reading scripture and journaling.
- discover my spiritual gift(s).
- identify a group or class that meets my next step on the discipleship journey.
- meet with someone to find a place to serve in ministry.
- make an informed decision about my next step on the discipleship pathway.

Class Commitments
I commit to uphold three simple rules:

1. Be on time.

2. Complete the readings and activities for the week.

3. Contact the leader if you are unable to attend class.

Member Vows
I vow to uphold the church by my:

- *Prayers* – Practicing the spiritual disciplines of prayer and Scripture meditation.

- *Presence* – Celebrating God's presence in worship and experiencing Christian community in a small group or class.

- *Gifts* – Practicing Christian stewardship by practicing or growing toward the spiritual discipline of tithing.

- *Service* – Participating in God's transformation of the world by discovering my spiritual gifts and participating in God's work through the ministry of the church.

- *Witness* – Inviting others to experience God's love and become disciples of Jesus.

_____
Signature

_____
Date

Church History Tree

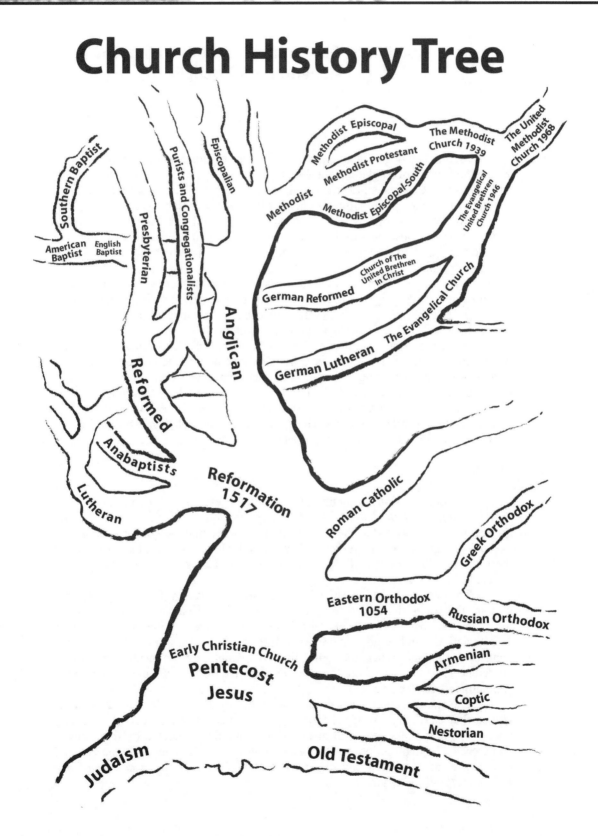

Introduction to The United Methodist Church: History, Structure, and Beliefs

History

Methodism began as an eighteenth-century spiritual renewal movement within the Church of England. John Wesley, a priest in the Church of England, and his brother Charles, a priest and songwriter, are most often identified as the founders of the movement, although neither intended to start a new church.

The Wesleys emphasized scriptural holiness, vital piety, and acts of justice and compassion. Observers derided the Wesleys and their followers for being so "methodical" in their discipline and spiritual practice. The Wesleys embraced this description as their moniker, and the Methodist movement was born.

Once the movement crossed the ocean to colonial America, it took on a life of its own, becoming The Methodist Episcopal Church in 1784. Eventually, the Wesleys' governing authority waned over the American Methodists, even though their spiritual and doctrinal influence remained.

In the nineteenth century, the growth of The Methodist Episcopal Church paralleled the emergence of another Christian movement in the United States, The Evangelical United Brethren Church. The EUB Church was born from a merger of The Evangelical Church and The United Brethren Church, with strong roots in the Midwest and the Northeast. Over time, the Methodist and EUB churches recognized their similarities in doctrine, practice, and church organization. In 1968, these churches became The United Methodist Church.

Structure

The organizational structure of the United Methodist Church is established in *The United Methodist Book of Discipline* much as the United States government was outlined in the Constitution. Both are made up of three branches: executive, legislative, and judicial. The United Methodist Church's version of these three is the Council of Bishops, the General Conference, and the Judicial Council.

The church is also organized in a hierarchical system. Beginning from the bottom, the smallest units in the UMC are its lay and pastoral members. Each local church has an annual "local church charge conference" to elect representatives and guide them in fulfilling their missions. Churches are connected to each other to form districts, which are connected in annual conferences. At the annual conferences, an assigned bishop announces ministerial appointments for the year.

The annual conferences are grouped into jurisdictions; there are five in the United States. At the top of this chain is the General Conference, which meets once every four years, made up of lay people and clergy elected by their annual conferences. Its main purpose is to vote on church law. If enacted by the General Conference, the proposed laws are published in *The Book of Discipline of The United Methodist Church*.

Beliefs

Key Beliefs and Values

- We believe that salvation is found in and through Jesus Christ.
- We believe that the Bible is the word of God and the primary authority for Christian life and faith. While we believe the Bible is true, we do not believe every verse of the Bible must be interpreted literally. Methodists interpret Scripture through reason, tradition, and experience.
- We believe in justification by grace through faith. We believe in personal holiness and social action.
- We believe in living by grace and striving for holiness–to become like Christ.
- We believe in the balance of heart and head.
- We believe in providence on the one hand and human freedom on the other.
- We value tradition and are willing to embrace change.
- We believe that God's redemptive love is realized in human life by the activity of the Holy Spirit.
- We believe that we are part of Christ's universal church as we become conformed to Christ.
- We recognize the kingdom of God as both a present and a future reality.
- While affirming the faith we share in common with all other Christians, we also affirm the unique emphasis the Wesleyan tradition places on the love and grace of God.
- We believe the sacraments of baptism and Holy Communion are means by which the intangible reality of God's grace touches our lives in tangible ways.

The Trinity

United Methodists believe in a trinitarian God in keeping with Christian tradition. This means that we believe in one God made known to us as Father, Son, and Holy Spirit. The Father, or God Almighty, is the creative God who authored all life. The Son is the redeeming God who became fully human—Jesus Christ. The Holy Spirit is the sustaining God who nurtures individuals and communities.

Salvation

We believe that as God's creations, we are meant to live in a holy covenant with this trinitarian God. However, we also teach that we have broken this covenant by our sins, and we are forgiven by God's love and saving grace in Jesus Christ. We believe that Jesus was God on earth (the product of a virgin conception) in the form of a man who was crucified for the sins of all people, and who was physically resurrected to bring us the hope of eternal life. We believe that salvation is found in and through Jesus Christ. We believe in justification by faith through grace.

Grace

United Methodists place a strong emphasis on the love and grace of God. We believe that God's grace is an active part of every human's life from the moment of birth (*prevenient grace),* to the individual's saving experience of God through Jesus Christ (*justifying grace),* and throughout the rest of his or her life in Christian discipleship (*sanctifying grace)*. The grace of God is perceived by people through the work of the Holy Spirit in their lives and in their world.

The Bible

We believe that the Bible is the word of God and the primary authority for Christian life and faith. While we believe the Bible is true, we do not believe every verse of the Bible must be interpreted literally. Methodists interpret Scripture through reason, tradition, and experience. We uphold the Bible as the primary witness of the nature and activity of God and God's relationship to humanity. Our canon, or official collection of biblical material, is the same as other Protestant churches–sixty-six books (thirty-nine in the Old Testament, twenty-seven in the New Testament).

The Sacraments of Baptism and Holy Communion

Along with other Protestant churches, The United Methodist Church affirms two sacraments as "the outward and visible sign" of the grace of God in human experience: baptism and Holy Communion. We believe these sacraments are means by which the intangible reality of God's grace touches our lives in tangible ways.

Baptism is the sign of the grace of God that claims us as God's own children. We believe it is the beginning point of our spiritual journey. Baptism is the outward and visible sign of the inward and spiritual grace of God's work of love in an individual's life even before he or she is able to understand it or choose to accept it. We call this "prevenient grace." Baptism is a ceremony in which a person is anointed with water to symbolize being brought into the community of faith by the grace of God. Baptism is celebrated in worship because the person being baptized is welcomed into the community of faith.

While some denominations choose to wait until a person is able to couple baptism with understanding and public profession of faith, we invite the parents and the church to affirm this grace on behalf of the child as they pledge to raise the child in the faith until the time that the child is able to accept God's grace for himself or herself, usually at the time of confirmation, which is between sixth and eighth grades in most churches. A candidate for Holy Baptism or his or her sponsors may choose any of the traditional ways baptism is administered: sprinkling, pouring, or immersion. The most common method in United Methodist Churches is sprinkling.

We believe that Holy Communion, also known as The Lord's Supper or Eucharist, celebrates the grace of God that is present with us as we share in the body (the bread) and the blood (grape juice or wine) of Christ. As participants eat and drink, they symbolically receive Christ's body (the bread) and blood (typically juice in United Methodist churches).

We observe an open invitation for Communion, which means one need not be a member of a United Methodist congregation in order to observe the Eucharist. The only requirement is a personal desire to experience the grace of God revealed through Jesus Christ. Often parents wonder whether it is appropriate for their children to receive Communion. Since there is no official doctrine on the matter, parents are free to decide at what point their children are able to understand its meaning and significance, and we welcome children of any age to receive the sacrament.

Providence and Free Will

United Methodists don't necessarily believe in a micromanaging God who directly controls everything that happens. While holding to a high view of the sovereignty of God, we don't believe that "God has a reason for everything." Rather, we believe that God loves us enough to give us the freedom to reject that love and to experience the consequences of that freedom. At the same time, God is relentlessly at work to fulfill God's saving purpose for us while never abrogating the freedom planted within us. God intends for everyone--not just a predestined few--to receive God's saving love and redeeming grace in Jesus Christ.

Personal Holiness and Social Action

United Methodists believe in living by grace and striving for holiness—to become like Christ–in both personal piety and social action. We agree with the writer of the epistle of James that faith without works is dead. The inner transformation of the heart must be expressed through social transformation of the world in which we live. Personal holiness is the way we breathe in; social holiness is the way we breathe out.

As a result, United Methodists place a great emphasis on service to others, outreach, and evangelism as the expressions of God's love at work in the world. We have a strong legacy in ministries of mercy and justice. John Wesley gave the early Methodists three guiding principles for their lives, which he called "General Rules" (paraphrased from *The United Methodist Book of Discipline,* 2004, pp. 73-74):

- Do no harm by avoiding evil.
- Do good in every possible way.
- Be faithful in the practices of Christian discipline.

Methodist hospitals, schools, relief agencies, and numerous other organizations seek to alleviate human suffering, promote peace and justice, and improve the welfare of the global community. For more information about how The United Methodist Church is involved in missions around the world, see the website of the General Board of Global Ministries (www.gbgm-umc.org).

The Social Principles is the document that best reflects the ongoing dialogue within the United Methodist community in matters of social, economic, and political importance. The Social Principles is an expression of the church's effort to discern biblically, traditionally, experientially, and rationally the Methodist stance on the controversial issues of the day. To find more information and to read the full text of the Social Principles, visit www.umc.org.

Creeds of the Faith

The Apostles' Creed in *The United Methodist Hymnal* is the affirmation of faith most widely used by United Methodists. The Apostles' Creed derives its name from its use in the Christian church from as early as A.D. 150 and the early belief that it was used by the apostles. Beginning in the third century, this creed was used at baptisms by the Roman Catholic Church. Through the years it has been used widely by both Roman Catholics and Protestants as the formative statement of the faith into which Christians are baptized (from *The United Methodist Hymnal*, 1989, p. 881):

The Apostles' Creed

I believe in God, the Father Almighty,
Maker of heaven and earth;

And in Jesus Christ, his only Son our Lord;
who was conceived by the Holy Spirit,
born of the Virgin Mary,
suffered under Pontius Pilate,
was crucified, dead, and buried;
the third day he rose from the dead;
he ascended into heaven,
and sitteth at the right hand of the Father Almighty;
from thence he shall come again to judge the quick and the dead.

I believe in the Holy Spirit,
the holy catholic* church,
the communion of saints,
the forgiveness of sins,
the resurrection of the body,
and the life everlasting. Amen.

*catholic—small "c" means universal. So it means we believe in the universal church, rather than in the Catholic denomination.

The Nicene Creed is frequently used as an affirmation of faith in United Methodist worship services. The Nicene Creed is the historic statement of belief of the Christian faith devised by the Council of Nicaea, convened in A.D. 325 by the Emperor Constantine in the city of Nicaea, located in what is now northwest Turkey. The Creed was revised in 381 by the Council of Constantinople. The Nicene Creed set forth the key affirmations concerning the Christian faith and served as a guide in combating heretical or false teaching. The other important distinction is that it is communal; it is what "we" believe as opposed to what "I" believe, as in the Apostle's Creed. Following the Apostles' Creed, it is the second oldest creed of the Christian faith (from *The United Methodist Hymnal,* 1989, p. 881):

The Nicene Creed

We believe in one God,
    the Father, the Almighty,
    maker of heaven and earth,
    of all that is, seen and unseen.

We believe in one Lord, Jesus Christ,
    the only Son of God,
    eternally begotten of the Father,
    God from God, Light from Light,
    true God from true God,
    begotten, not made,
    of one Being with the Father;
    through him all things were made.
    For us and for our salvation
        he came down from heaven,
        was incarnate of the Holy Spirit and the Virgin Mary
        and became truly human.
        For our sake he was crucified under Pontius Pilate;
        he suffered death and was buried.
        On the third day he rose again
        in accordance with the Scriptures;
        he ascended into heaven
        and is seated at the right hand of the Father.
        He will come again in glory
        to judge the living and the dead,
        and his kingdom will have no end.

We believe in the Holy Spirit, the Lord, the giver of life,
    who proceeds from the Father and the Son,
    who with the Father and the Son
        is worshiped and glorified,
    who has spoken through the prophets.
    We believe in one holy catholic* and apostolic church.
    We acknowledge one baptism
        for the forgiveness of sins.
    We look for the resurrection of the dead,
        and the life of the world to come. Amen.

*universal church

The Mission of The United Methodist Church is "to make disciples of Jesus Christ for the transformation of the world."

Recommended Resources
- o Thomas S. McNally, *Questions and Answers About the United Methodist Church*, Abingdon Press, 1995 [see http://www.cokesbury.com/forms/ProductDetail.aspx?pid=438810]
- o Belton Joyner, *The "Unofficial" United Methodist Handbook*, Abingdon Press, 2007 [see http://www.cokesbury.com/forms/ProductDetail.aspx?pid=446592]
- o Introductory brochures on Communion and United Methodists, Baptism and United Methodists, It's All About God's Grace, Membership and United Methodists, The People of The United Methodist Church, and What's So Great about Being United Methodist? [see http://www.cokesbury.com/forms/ProductDetail.aspx?pid=855745]
- o http://UMC.org
- o http://gbod.org

Mission, Values, Strategy, and Vision

(SAMPLE—Modify for Your Church)

Our Mission

The mission of (church name) is (making God's love real/or insert your mission statement). (Church name) is a community of people committed to Jesus Christ, empowered by the Holy Spirit, united in the love of God, and called to make that love real to others.

The reason (church name) exists is to (make God's love real/or restate your mission statement).

Core Values

Christ-Centered: Focused on the life, words, way, and Spirit of Jesus proclaimed in the New Testament.

Biblically-rooted: Encourages spiritually-alive, faithful study of the Bible using tools of devotion and scholarship that are appropriate to a diverse body of people.

Warm-hearted: A joyful, loving, laughing congregation that experiences the grace of God in Jesus Christ in personal and positive ways.

Open-minded: A place where people search, think, question, and honestly express their growing experience of the faith in an accepting and affirming atmosphere.

Mission-directed: Continuing the strong sense of mission which has been part of our identity, both in terms of mission to the city and mission in the world.

Connection-committed: As part of The United Methodist Church, we see ourselves as a leader/supporter of the global ministries in which we share.

These values define who we are and how we participate in community together.

Our Strategy

The (church name) faith community is becoming a congregation of people who:

Invite people to experience the love of God and become disciples of Jesus Christ.

Equip disciples to be agents of God's reconciling love in the world.

Care for one another in Christian community.

Send disciples as servants of Christ to participate in God's transformation of the world.

These strategies are the ways that we move toward our vision and accomplish our mission.

Our Vision

As we (make God's love real/or insert your vision statement), the Holy Spirit will be:

(1) Transforming lives, (2) Creating Christian community, (3) Healing the city and the world.

As the (church name) (makes God's love real/or insert your vision statement), lives from its core values, and becomes people who (Invite, Equip, Care, and Send), the Holy Spirit will fulfill our vision of (transforming lives, creating Christian community, and healing the city and the world/or insert your vision statement).

NEXT STEPS CARD

Name: _____Phone_____ Email_____

Address: _____

1. _____ I'd be interested in talking with someone about a small group, Sunday school class, or Bible study.

2. _____ I'm ready to take the next step in the path of discipleship and want to take *A Disciple's Path*.

3. _____ I am interested in talking with someone about my spiritual journey and where God might be calling me at this time in my life.

4. _____ I'd like to begin to serve in a ministry area.

5. _____ Right now, my best next step is to attend church regularly, prior to getting involved in a class or ministry.

Please fill out at the end of the coffee.

---cut here--

NEXT STEPS CARD

Name: _____Phone_____ Email_____

Address: _____

1. _____ I'd be interested in talking with someone about a small group, Sunday school class, or Bible study.

2. _____ I'm ready to take the next step in the path of discipleship and want to take *A Disciple's Path*.

3. _____ I am interested in talking with someone about my spiritual journey and where God might be calling me at this time in my life.

4. _____ I'd like to begin to serve in a ministry area.

5. _____ Right now, my best next step is to attend church regularly, prior to getting involved in a class or ministry.

Please fill out at the end of the coffee.

PERSONAL INFORMATION FORM
(Please Print)

Last
Name_____

First
Name _____

Middle
Name_____
(Initial not sufficient)

Name you go by _____ Maiden Name_____

Mr. Miss Mrs. Ms. Dr. Rev.   Military Rank_____   Other Title _____ _____
(circle one)

Street Address _____

City _____ Zip _____ Home Phone (   )_____

Cell Phone (   ) _____

E-Mail Address (for receiving church information) _____

Mailing Address if Different from Above_____

Birth Date:_____ Place of Birth _____

Marital Status _____ Anniversary Date (if married) _____

Occupation _____ Business Phone (   )_____

Place of Employment _____ Fax Number _____

Have you been Baptized? Yes __ No __ If yes, when? Denomination_____

Are you currently on the membership roll of any church ?_____   Yes _____ No _____

Church Name: _____

Church Address (Street/City/Zip): _____

If joining upon completion of *A Disciple's Path*, which worship service will you attend for reception of new members (time/location):

_____

Other individuals in household *(please complete for all family members even if they are not joining at this time)*.

NAME	RELATIONSHIP
_____	_____
_____	_____
_____	_____
_____	_____

For office use:

Date Received:_____ Joined by_____

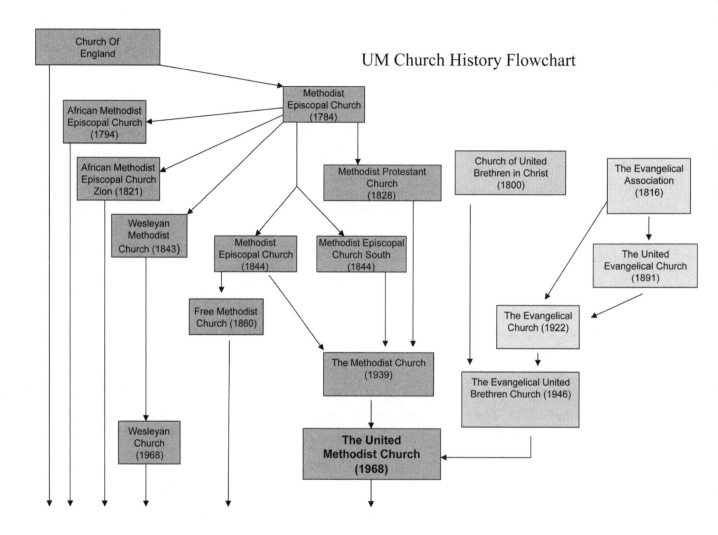

UM Church History Flowchart

The United Methodist Church Structure and Organization

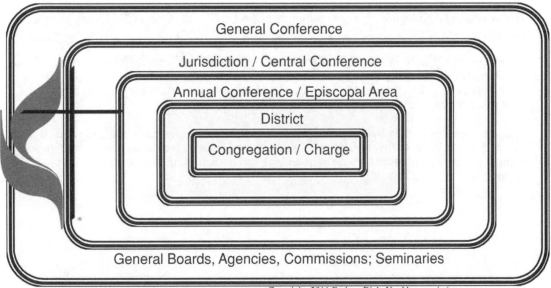

Copyright 2011 Barbara Dick. Used by permission.

Congregation / Charge: Individual or small group of local congregations served by appointed clergy and elected lay leadership. Opportunities for serving needs of local community through gifted ministry.

District: Geographic area with appointed clergy superintendent; opportunities for collaborative leadership and resourcing.

Annual Conference / Episcopal Area: An annual conference is both a geographic area of congregations and districts, with elected bishop and resource facilities and staff AND the annual meeting of lay and clergy members of the annual conference, which sets vision, budget, and policy. An episcopal area may be made up of one or more annual conferences (similar to church and charge).

Central Conference: Global areas of congregations, with elected bishop and resource facilities and staff (West Germany, Poland, Philippines, etc.).

Jurisdiction: Geographic area of annual conferences. Jurisdictional conference, held every four years, elects and appoints bishops and sets annual conference boundaries. There are five jurisdictions in the U.S.

General Conference: Global denomination of annual conferences and central conferences, with resource agencies and commissions that serve the entire church AND the meeting of the global church that occurs every four years to set policy and polity for the denomination.
- Structure is similar to U.S. government – General Conference is top legislative body; nine-member Judicial Council is "supreme court"; Council of Bishops is similar to executive branch (from umc.org).
- General Conference legislates, sets policy.
- 600–1000 delegates + agency staff, professors, college of bishops, council of bishops, staff, students, Judicial Council.
- Rewrites *Book of Discipline*. New *Book of Resolutions*. Can update *Book of Worship*, *Hymnal*.
- General Boards and Agencies serve and take action take action on behalf of the entire church.
- Seminaries and UM-related Colleges are certified by the church to educate elders and deacons for ordination.

What Church Membership Means

The vows we take when we become a member of a United Methodist Church are grouped into three categories:

1. Profession of faith in Jesus Christ to become part of Christ's universal church.
2. Declaration of loyalty to The United Methodist Church in particular.
3. A pledge to participate faithfully in this local congregation through prayers, presence, gifts, service, and witness.

The vows we make to participate in the ministries of the church are not multiple choice. Just as Jesus calls us to love God and neighbor through heart, soul, mind, and strength, so being a disciple involves the whole self, and we strive to commit our entire lives to God through our

> Prayers
> Presence
> Gifts
> Service
> Witness

Prayers: *Prayer and Scripture Meditation*

Spending time in prayer each day, and studying and reflecting on the Bible to experience the living Word of hope in the written word of Scripture.

Presence: *Corporate Worship and Small-group Community*

Celebrating God's presence in worship with a faith community, and experiencing Christian community in a small group to pray, learn, and grow together.

Gifts: *Financial Generosity*

Practicing Christian stewardship through the biblical discipline of tithing.

Service: *Spiritual Gifts and Gifts-based Service*

Discovering our spiritual gifts and participating in God's work through the ministry of the church.

Witness: *Invitational Evangelism*

Inviting others to experience God's love and become disciples of Jesus Christ.

Mind Mapping Guidelines

1. In the center of a blank page, draw a colorful image representing your subject.

2. Branch off from the image, drawing lines to connect other ideas—words and images. Use key words, printing each on its own line. Be sure to print the letters, rather than use cursive writing, to make the words easy to read. Try to keep one word per line, letting each word spark new ideas and images.

3. Vary the ways you link ideas, using highlighters, codes, arrows, or other techniques. Try to use at least three different colors.

4. Your map will develop a natural "hierarchy" of ideas, with the more primary ideas near the center.

5. Take note of any similar ideas or images in your map. This may signify an underlying or significant concept.

Who Said That? A Bible Quiz

Identify the speaker and the passage. The language used in your version of the Bible may differ from what is shown here. You will earn 1 point for each correct answer.

1. "Honour thy father and thy mother." (KJV)

   Who said that?_____

   Bible Location: _____

2. "When I was a child, I spoke like a child; I thought like a child; I reasoned like a child. When I became an adult I put an end to childish ways." (NRSV)

   Who said that?_____

   Bible Location: _____

3. "Lord, how many times shall I forgive my brother or sister who sins against me? Up to seven times?"
   Jesus answered, "I tell you, not seven times, but seventy-seven times." (NIV)

   Who asked the question?_____

   Bible Location: _____

4. "Consider the lilies, how they grow: they neither toil nor spin; yet I tell you even Solomon in all his glory was not clothed like one of these." (NRSV)

   Who said that?_____

   Bible Location: _____

5. "Before I formed you in the womb I knew you,
      before you were born I set you apart;
      I appointed you as a prophet to the nations." (TNIV)

   Who is God speaking to? _____

   Bible Location: _____

6. "Am I my brother's keeper?" (NRSV)

   Who said that?_____

   Bible Location: _____

7. "If we claim, 'We don't have any sin,' we deceive ourselves and the truth is not in us. But if we confess our sins, he is faithful and just to forgive us our sins and cleanse us from everything we've done wrong. . . . "

   ". . . if you do sin, we have an advocate with the Father, Jesus Christ the righteous one. He is God's way of dealing with our sins, not only ours but the sins of the whole world." (CEB)

   Who said that?_____

   Bible Location: _____

8. "His winnowing fork is in his hand, and he will clear his threshing floor, gathering his wheat into the barn and burning up the chaff with unquenchable fire." (NIV)

   Who said that?_____

   Bible Location: _____

9. "Whither thou goest, I will go. Whither thou lodgest, I will lodge: Thy people will be my people, and thy God my God." (KJV)

   Who said that?_____

   To whom? _____

   Bible Location: _____

10. "For what shall it profit a man, if he gains the whole world, and loses his own soul?" (NKJV)

    Who said that?_____

    Bible Location: _____

11. "And now faith, hope, and love abide, these three; and the greatest of these is love." (NRSV)

    Who said that?_____

    Bible Location: _____

12. "Blessed art thou among women, and blessed is the fruit of thy womb." (KJV)

    Who said that?_____

    Bible Location: _____

13. ". . . but as for me and my house, we will serve the LORD." (NRSV)

    Who said that?_____

    Bible Location: _____

14. ". . . they will beat their swords into iron plows
    and their spears into pruning tools.
  Nation will not take up sword against nation;
    they will no longer learn how to make war." (CEB)

Who said that?_____

Bible Location: _____

Extra Credit. Since 1908 Gideons International, or The Gideons, has placed over 1.7 billion Bibles in hotel rooms, including some 709 million in 2009.

What version of the Bible is the Gideon Bible? _____

Who Said That? A Bible Quiz Answer Key

Identify the speaker and the passage. The language used in your version of the Bible may differ from what is shown here. You will earn 1 point for each correct answer.

1. "Honour thy father and thy mother." (KJV)

   Who said that? **God**

   Bible Location: **Exodus 20:12**

2. "When I was a child, I spoke like a child; I thought like a child; I reasoned like a child. When I became an adult I put an end to childish ways." (NRSV)

   Who said that? **Paul**

   Bible Location: **1 Corinthians 13:11**

3. "Lord, how many times shall I forgive my brother or sister who sins against me? Up to seven times?"
   Jesus answered, "I tell you, not seven times, but seventy-seven times." (NIV)

   Who asked the question? **Peter**

   Bible Location: **Matthew 18:21-22**

4. "Consider the lilies, how they grow: they neither toil nor spin; yet I tell you even Solomon in all his glory was not clothed like one of these." (NRSV)

   Who said that? **Jesus**

   Bible Location: **Luke 12:27**

5. "Before I formed you in the womb I knew you,
   before you were born I set you apart;
   I appointed you as a prophet to the nations." (TNIV)

   Who is God speaking to? **Jeremiah**

   Bible Location: **Jeremiah 1:5**

6. "Am I my brother's keeper?" (NRSV)

   Who said that? **Cain**

   Bible Location: **Genesis 4:9**

7. "If we claim, 'We don't have any sin,' we deceive ourselves and the truth is not in us. But if we confess our sins, he is faithful and just to forgive us our sins and cleanse us from everything we've done wrong. . . . "

   ". . . if you do sin, we have an advocate with the Father, Jesus Christ the righteous one. He is God's way of dealing with our sins, not only ours but the sins of the whole world." (CEB)

   Who said that? **John, son of Zebedee** _____

   Bible Location: **1 John 1:8–2:2** _____

8. "His winnowing fork is in his hand, and he will clear his threshing floor, gathering his wheat into the barn and burning up the chaff with unquenchable fire." (NIV)

   Who said that? **John the Baptist** _____

   Bible Locations (2): **Matthew 3:12 and Luke 3:17 (Luke varies slightly)**

9. "Whither thou goest, I will go; and where thou lodgest, I will lodge: Thy people shall be my people, and thy God my God." (KJV)

   Who said that? **Ruth** _____

   To whom? **Naomi** _____

   Bible Location: **Ruth 1:16** _____

10. "For what will it profit a man if he gains the whole world, and loses his own soul?" (NKJV)

    Who said that? **Jesus** _____

    Bible Location: **Mark 8:36** _____

11. "And now faith, hope, and love abide, these three; and the greatest of these is love." (NRSV)

    Who said that? **Paul** _____

    Bible Location: **1 Corinthians 13:13** _____

12. "Blessed art thou among women, and blessed is the fruit of thy womb." (KJV)

    Who said that? **Elizabeth, Mary's cousin** _____

    Bible Location: **Luke 1:42** _____

13. ". . . but as for me and my house, we will serve the LORD." (NRSV)

    Who said that? **Joshua** _____

    Bible Location: **Joshua 24:15** _____

14. ". . . they will beat their swords into iron plows
    and their spears into pruning tools.
  Nation will not take up sword against nation;
    they will no longer learn how to make war." (CEB)

    Who said that? **Isaiah (speaking God's words)** _____

    Bible Location: **Isaiah 2:4**

    _____

Extra Credit. Since 1908 Gideons International, or The Gideons, has placed over 1.7 billion Bibles in hotel rooms*, including some 709 million in 2009.

    What version of the Bible is the Gideon Bible? **The King James Version (KJV), unless the hotel or recipient requests a modern language version. Then The New King James Version (NKJV), or "Modern English Version" (MEV) is distributed.**

* The Gideons also distribute Bibles to the military, hospitals, nursing homes, prisons, and students. Gideon Bibles have been distributed in 94 languages and 194 countries.

Small-group Overview

Name: _____ Date: _____

Phone(s): _____ E-mail: _____

I would like to become involved in the following small-group communities:

_____

_____

(Cut or tear here and return top half to class facilitator.)

Small-group Community Options

(NOTE: Customize by replacing the following listing with small-group options available in your congregation. Add pages as necessary.)

Sunday School (ongoing): Groups vary in content and study. Some are organized by age, life stage, or simply by topic.

Beginnings (12 weeks): A small group that explores the basics of Christianity in a relaxed, nurturing atmosphere.

Financial Peace University (13 weeks): A program that teaches us how to make grace-filled decisions about money.

Short-term Bible study (6-8 weeks): A moderate-level class that explores portions of the Bible.

Disciple Bible Study 1 (34 weeks): High-commitment study that will help build the foundation for your study of the Bible.

Wesley Group (ongoing): 6–14 people who come together to build relationships through encouragement, accountability, guidance, and prayer so that all members experience life-transformation through Christ.

Covenant Group (ongoing): 7 people who regularly meet together to hold themselves mutually accountable for their discipleship. They are guided by a covenant that they write, shaped by the discipleship pathway. A covenant group is not where our discipleship happens, but where we make sure it happens.

Other ideas: Choir(s), United Methodist Men, United Methodist Women, Committees, Teams, Boards, Work Groups, and Planning Groups. All of these experiences offer opportunities for spiritual growth along the discipleship pathway.

Writing a Money Autobiography

Introduction

Writing a money autobiography is a challenging and illuminating process that can be crucial to our ability to understand ourselves as Christian stewards. While stewardship is about more than money, it certainly never concerns less than money; and in our modern culture, money defines, to a great extent, who we are, how we live, and what we believe. For the largest part of our society, it is impossible to envision a life without money.

Our relationship with money is a timeless issue. Jesus speaks more about money than any other topic, with the exception of the kingdom of God. More than prayer; more than grace; more than sin; more than salvation, love, or forgiveness, Jesus teaches and preaches about our relationship to money. Obviously, Jesus understood that only through a healthy self-understanding of this critical issue could a man or woman rise to his or her full potential. Once Christian stewards prove themselves trustworthy over fiscal matters, they are ready to address matters more sacred and spiritual in nature.

What is a Money Autobiography?

A money autobiography is a reflection on the role money has played in our lives. We explore the past to see how our attitudes and assumptions about money and material possessions developed. We analyze the present to see how well we manage (or are managed by) money. We look toward the future to envision the role money will play in taking us where we want to go. A Money Autobiography can assist us in the process of personal development, enabling us to understand how money can help or hinder us in our journey to become who God intends us to be.

A money autobiography can be any length, but a good target to shoot for is three to five pages. Questions are provided to stimulate thought and provoke response. Feelings are as important as thoughts and facts. Think not only of your responses to the questions; also pay attention to how your responses make you feel. Re-experience some of the money events of your past and present life, and search these events for meaning.

This exercise is for your use only. Its purpose is to benefit your Christian walk and spiritual development. There is great personal benefit in the exercise of organizing and expressing your thoughts, feelings, and insights about money in your life. No one will see your money autobiography unless you choose to share it.

Using the Questions for Reflection

Read through the questions for reflection and respond to those that catch your attention or elicit a strong visceral response. Don't try to answer everything—you could write 200 pages and still not be finished! Jot down short, concise answers as you read the questions; then return to specific answers to reflect on their meaning. You may want to use these questions as daily reflections for a journal or longer-term writing project.

Questions for Reflection

What is your happiest memory in connection with money?

What is your unhappiest memory in connection with money?

What attitude did your mother hold toward money? your father?

What was your personal attitude toward money as a child? a teenager? a young adult?

Did you feel rich, poor, or something in between as a child?

Did you worry about money while you were growing up? Did your family?

As a child, where did your money come from? (allowance, chores, etc.)

Who governed how you would use your money? (save, spend, etc.)

Did you save as a child? as a teenager? If yes, for what did you save?

Did you give money to the church? Did your parents? Who taught you about giving?

Today, are you basically a saver or a spender?

Are you basically generous?

Do you feel financially secure?

Do you fear losing what you have?

Does money make you happy? Do you wish you had more? Would having less money make you less happy?

Do you ever feel guilty about money? How/Why?

What do you like best about money? What do you like least?

Do you consider yourself a wise money manager? Do you waste money? Do you get full value for the money your save/spend?

Which of the following words describe your feelings/attitudes about money?

power	security	hope	pleasure	love
identity	prestige	comfort	anxiety	gift
protection	need	value	burden	tool

Do you ever worry about money? In what ways?

Does your gender influence your attitudes about money? Do you think men and women view money differently? Why, and in what ways?

What are some gender stereotypes that you can think of concerning money? In what ways do you think they are valid?

Do you like to buy things for other people? When you eat out, do you pick up the check? For whom are you most likely to buy things?

Do you tend to be on the giving end or the receiving end more often in your life? How do you feel about it?

If you were struggling to make needs meet, would you accept the offer of financial help from a friend? a family member?

If you have money and another person has financial need, will you offer assistance?

As a rule, do you borrow money? Do you lend money to others?

Do you use credit cards? Do you carry a balance or pay in full each month?

Do you buy on time-payments? (cars, appliances, etc.)

Do you carry a mortgage on your house? How soon do you plan to pay it off?

Do you have a second mortgage/home equity loan? How soon do you plan to pay it off?

How much debt is reasonable to carry on a regular basis? (50%+ annual income, 25%, 15%, 10%, 5%, 0%)

Do you give regularly to church? What percentage of your income do you give? (1%, 2%, 3%, 5%, 10%, 15%+)

Do you clearly understand what the church does with your money?

Do you give to charities beyond the church?

Do you clearly understand how charities that you support spend your money?

How do you feel when charities call your home to ask for money? when they send requests through the mail?

How do you feel when you are approached on the street by someone asking for money?

Two-thirds of the world's population lives below the poverty level. How does this make you feel?

Who has a claim on the money you earn/save?

Do you consider yourself:

| affluent | comfortable | average | struggling | poor |

Have you written a will? Why, or why not?

What factors determine how you will divide your estate? Are you leaving money to a church, charity, or worthy cause?

The New Testament is clear that our individual wealth is to be used for the common good. What does this mean to you? Does anyone have a legitimate right to your wealth besides you?

How has your relationship with God been influenced by your relationship with money?

How has your relationship with money been influenced by your relationship with God?

In what ways does money create an obstacle to faithful Christian discipleship? In what ways does money make discipleship easier?

Is money an easy topic for you to talk about? Is there any area of personal finance that you don't like talking about?

Is money talk embarrassing for you? Why?

Does money talk in the church make you uncomfortable? Why?

Which response most accurately describes your feelings about fundraising campaigns in the church:

> They inspire me.
> They make me angry.
> I ignore them.
> They bore me.
> They make me want to give more.
> They make me want to give less.
> They don't influence me one way or the other.

Why do you feel the way you do about fundraising/financial campaigns in the church?

Is your sense of self-esteem related to the amount of money you have? Do you feel that people with more money feel better about themselves than people with little money?

In what ways is money a spiritual issue? What can you do to improve your relationship with money? In what ways can God help you with your relationship with money and material wealth?

Money Matters

My Glossary of Financial Generosity

Abundance:_____

_____

_____

Enough: _____

_____

_____

Generosity: _____

_____

_____

Need: _____

_____

_____

Ownership: _____

_____

_____

Riches:_____

_____

_____

Stewardship:_____

_____

_____

Treasure:_____

_____

_____

Plain Rules for Generosity: My Plan to Grow in Financial Giving

1. "Generosity begins with God." We give in loving response to God's gifts to us.
   - What have I received from God that makes me feel so good I can't wait to share it with others?

   _____

   _____

   _____

2. "Generosity is essential. . . . Our use of money undergoes a fundamental transformation when we stop asking how much of our wealth we will give to God and start asking how much of God's wealth we will keep for ourselves."
   - How much of God's wealth do I need to keep for myself?

   _____

   _____

   _____

3. "Generosity is intentional." Review the 10-10-80 principle.
   - What steps do I plan to take to move toward this goal?

   _____

   _____

   _____

   - What is stopping me from approaching this goal?

   _____

   _____

   _____

4. "Generosity grows with practice." As we learn to give we learn to love giving and want to give more.
   - What will I do tomorrow to take the first step in growing my practice of generosity in financial giving?

   _____

   _____

   _____

5. "Generosity is joyful." When you give a gift chosen with care, it makes you feel wonderful.
   - What are the first fruits of my labor? How will I offer them to God?

   _____

   _____

   _____

- How do I plan to make God my treasure?

_____

_____

_____

6. "Generosity results in blessing." Giving for the sake of giving is reflected in the lives of those who receive and those who give.
   - What blessings have been made possible because of my giving to and through the church?

_____

_____

_____

*Quotations are from *A Disciple's Path Companion Reader*, Chapter 4

START HERE: AFTER PRAYERFUL CONSIDERATION, I WILL SERVE AS INDICATED BELOW AND INVITE OTHERS TO BECOME DISCIPLES OF JESUS CHRIST.

Household Member Name 1: (please print) _____

Email Address: _____

Household Member Name 2: (please print) _____

Email Address: _____

IN ADDITION TO SERVING, I WILL GROW SPIRITUALLY BY COMMITTING TO...

		Attend evangelism classes/workshops
		Attend prayer classes/workshops
		Attend Bible study classes/workshops
		Attend worship _____ Sundays in the next 12 months
		Develop a pattern of daily prayer
		Develop a pattern of daily scripture reflection
		Participate in a small group, Bible study, or Sunday school group. Name group/study of interest:
		Share my faith story (e.g., verbally with others, in articles or workshops, on video, etc.)

GIFTS-BASED SERVICE

Please mark those areas of service for which you are ready to commit, or re-commit, to serve.

ADMINISTRATIVE SUPPORT MINISTRIES

		Bulletin preparation
		General administrative assistance
		Receptionist

ADULT EDUCATION MINISTRIES

		Adult education team
		Bible study facilitator
		Discipleship group facilitator
		Financial management class facilitator
		One-time event coordinator
		Other small-group facilitator. Name the group:
		Short-term study facilitator
		Sunday school facilitator

MEDIA CENTER / BOOKSTORE / COFFEE SHOP

		Media center/bookstore volunteer
		Coffee shop volunteer

CHILDREN'S MINISTRIES

Family Ministries

		Family discipleship group facilitator
		New baby team

Miscellaneous Ministries

		Administrative volunteer
		Special events planning team
		Vacation Bible School

Sunday/Wednesday Ministries

		Greeter/registration team
		Large-group leader
		Music leader
		Nursery volunteer
		Small-group leader
		Resources/supplies team
		Tech team

COMMUNICATIONS MINISTRIES

		Communications team
		Online communications (web, blog)
		Pew folder team
		Photography ministry
		Newsletter writer/contributor/production assistance

COMMITMENT CARD

CONGREGATIONAL CARE MINISTRIES

Prayer Ministries

		Prayer team

Transportation Ministries

		Transportation to medical appointments
		Tansportation to worship

Visitation Ministries

		Hospital visitor
		Visit the home bound/those in assisted living facilities

Other Care Ministries

		Meal preparation for persons/families needing assistance

CONNECTING MINISTRIES

		A Disciple's Path facilitator
		Attendance taker ministry
		First-time guest connector (contact and follow-up)
		Inactive member connector (contact and follow-up)
		New member connector (helps connect to classes/ministries)
		New member lunch host
		Pastor's coffee coordinator

FACILITIES MAINTENANCE MINISTRIES

		Facilities maintenance and setup team

FINANCE MINISTRIES

		Financial statements team
		Offering counter and depositor

FOOD SERVICE MINISTRIES

		Special events meal preparation
		Special events server
		Wednesday night dinner preparation
		Wednesday night dinner table preparation and clean up
		Wednesday night dinner ticket sales

HELP!

		I need assistance finding my place to serve

HOSPITALITY MINISTRIES

		Campus greeter
		Campus tour guide
		Evangelism class facilitator
		Medical first responder
		Parking lot greeter
		Usher team

LEADERSHIP

		I would like to learn more about leadership at (church name).

HOW TO COMPLETE THIS FORM

- Please confirm or print your name, eamail address and phone number on the top of this form.
- On page 2, under the "Financial Generosity" section, print your name, address and phone number.
- The "Financial Generosity" section will be separated for privacy purposes upon submission.
- The form can accommodate information for two household members as necessary (Household Member 1, Household Member 2).
- Please mark those areas of service for which you are ready to commit, or re-commit, to serve.
- Someone will contact you regarding your service commitment(s) and orientation/training dates. A separate letter will be mailed about financial commitments.
- Return this completed form to your *A Disciple's Path* group leader.

Please mark those areas of service for which you are ready to commit, or re-commit, to serve.

MISCELLANEOUS

		Begin a new ministry
		Support team member for a new ministry
		Wherever the church needs me

MISSIONS AND OUTREACH MINISTRIES

Missions

		At-risk children/schools ministry
		Christmas/Easter planning teams
		Disaster relief and recovery
		Environmental ministry
		Food pantry/meals ministry
		Home maintenance and repair ministry
		Homeless ministry
		Mission and outreach ministry committee
		Ministries and service opportunities booklet production
		Tutoring

Local Community Agencies/Ministries

		Food bank
		Habitat for Humanity
		Health clinic
		Inner-city ministry
		Local food bank
		Meals on Wheels
		Mission
		Prison Ministry
		Red Cross
		Salvation Army

International Ministries

		Communicate with missionaries abroad
		Mission trip

MUSIC MINISTRIES - CONTEMPORARY

		Administrative support
		High school/middle school praise team coach
		High school praise team - instrumentalist or vocalist
		Middle school praise team - instrumentalist or vocalist
		Worship praise team - instrumentalist or vocalist

MUSIC MINISTRIES - TRADITIONAL

Administration

		Choir hospitality committee
		Choir prayer partners coordinator
		Choir robe care
		Music librarian

Adult Traditional Music

		Play an instrument or sing a solo during worship
		Handbell choir
		Sing with the choir

MUSIC MINISTRIES - TRADITIONAL

Children's Traditional Music

		Choir assistant/volunteer
		Children's musical volunteer (costumes, sets, choreography)
		Piano accompanist

WORSHIP AND MEDIA ARTS MINISTRIES

		Altar guild member (cares for linens and flowers)
		Communion - prepare / serve (circle one)
		Operate camera (if used)
		Operate computer/media
		Operate lights
		Operate sound
		Read Scripture in worship
		Technical director
		Worship design/creativity team

YOUTH MINISTRY

High School Youth Group

		Dinner preparation/pick up
		Small group leader

Middle School Youth Group

		Dinner preparation/pick up
		Small group leader

Sunday School

		High school Sunday school facilitator
		Middle school Sunday school facilitator

Other Opportunities

		Bible study leader
		Bus driver for special events (CDL required)
		Confirmation small-group facilitator
		Misson trip chaperone
		Off-site event chaperone
		On-site event chaperone

FINANCIAL GENEROSITY

I/we make the following financial commitments:

	General Ministry Fund
Per Week	
Per Month	
Other (please specify)	

___ This represents a commitment to give in proportion to my income, moving toward a tithe of 10%.

___ This represents a commitment to give at least a tithe of 10% to God's work through (church name).

___ Please send me information about monthly electronic funds transfer.

___ I would like information about including (church name) in my will.

Name(s):_____
Please print your name as it should appear on the offering envelope.

Address:_____

City, State, Zip:_____ Phone: _____

Gifted in Community
(All quotations from the NRSV)

Romans 12:3-8 (seven gifts)
For by the grace given to me I say to everyone among you not to think of yourself more highly than you ought to think, but to think with sober judgment, each according to the measure of faith that God has assigned. For as in one body we have many members, and not all the members have the same function, so we, who are many, are one body in Christ, and individually we are members one of another. We have gifts that differ according to the grace given to us: prophecy, in proportion to faith; ministry, in ministering; the teacher, in teaching; the exhorter, in exhortation; the giver, in generosity; the leader, in diligence; the compassionate, in cheerfulness.

Prophecy	Giving
Helps (Serving)	Leadership
Teaching	Mercy
Encouragement	

1 Corinthians 12:1-12 (nine gifts)
Now there are varieties of gifts, but the same Spirit; and there are varieties of services, but the same Lord; and there are varieties of activities, but it is the same God who activates all of them in everyone. To each is given the manifestation of the Spirit for the common good. To one is given through the Spirit the utterance of wisdom, and to another the utterance of knowledge according to the same Spirit, to another faith by the same Spirit, to another gifts of healing by the one Spirit, to another the working of miracles, to another prophecy, to another the discernment of spirits, to another various kinds of tongues, to another the interpretation of tongues. All these are activated by one and the same Spirit, who allots to each one individually just as the Spirit chooses.

Message of Wisdom	Prophecy
Message of Knowledge	Distinguishing of Spirits
Faith	Speaking in Tongues
Healing	Interpretation of Tongues
Miraculous Powers	

1 Corinthians 12:28 (four gifts)
Now you are the body of Christ and individually members of it. And God has appointed in the church first apostles, second prophets, third teachers; then deeds of power, then gifts of healing, forms of assistance, forms of leadership, various kinds of tongues.

Apostleship	Hospitality
Teaching	Administration

Ephesians 4:1-16 (five gifts)
The gifts he gave were that some would be apostles, some prophets, some evangelists, some pastors and teachers, to equip the saints for the work of ministry, for building up the body of Christ, until all of us come to the unity of the faith and of the knowledge of the Son of God, to maturity, to the measure of the full stature of Christ.

Apostleship	Pastors
Prophecy	Teachers
Evangelism	

Gifts-based Service Profile

Complete and turn in to your group leader.

Name: _____ Day Phone: _____

Evening Phone: _____ E-mail: _____

Have you taken the online spiritual gifts assessment? Yes / No

If not, please take the assessment at http://www.ministrymatters.com/spiritualgifts/ before continuing.

What was surprising or challenging to you in the results?

_____

_____

List your three top spiritual gifts (in order):

(1)_____ (2) _____ (3) _____

What skills/talents would you like to employ in ministry (education, employment, hobbies, interests, abilities)?

_____

What is your "holy discontent"? What do you see in the world that breaks your heart?

_____

_____

Are you currently using your gifts serving in the church? Yes / No

   If yes, where? _____

Are you currently using your gifts serving outside the church? Yes / No

   If yes, where? _____

What questions do you have about using your spiritual gifts in building up the body of Christ?

_____

_____

_____

In what areas of ministry would you like to use your gifts in serving the church?

_____

_____

_____

Spiritual Gifts Bingo

For each of the gifts on this sheet, identify a biblical character you believe possessed that gift. Be sure you can explain why the character fits the gift. In the middle (free) space, choose any gift from those listed in the Spiritual Gifts Descriptions in the *Daily Workbook* (including the three charismatic gifts) and share when and how Jesus manifested that gift.

Teaching	Hospitality	Evangelism
Apostleship	_____ (Any Gift) *Jesus Christ*	Message of Wisdom
Distinguishing of Spirits	Speaking in Tongues	Giving

Adapted from Dan Dick and Barbara Dick, *Equipped for Every Good Work* (Wipf & Stock, 2011); equippedforeverygoodwork.wordpress.com. Used by permission.

Spiritual Gifts Bingo

For each of the gifts on this sheet, identify a biblical character you believe possessed that gift. Be sure you can explain why the character fits the gift. In the middle (free) space, choose any gift from those listed in the Spiritual Gifts Descriptions in the *Daily Workbook* (including the three charismatic gifts) and share when and how Jesus manifested that gift.

Helps (Serving)	Faith	Giving
Encouragement	_____ (Any Gift) *Jesus Christ*	Teaching
Pastor-Teacher	Message of Knowledge	Tongues

Adapted from Dan Dick and Barbara Dick, *Equipped for Every Good Work* (Wipf & Stock, 2011); equippedforeverygoodwork.wordpress.com. Used by permission.

Spiritual Gifts Bingo

For each of the gifts on this sheet, identify a biblical character you believe possessed that gift. Be sure you can explain why the character fits the gift. In the middle (free) space, choose any gift from those listed in the Spiritual Gifts Descriptions in the *Daily Workbook* (including the three charismatic gifts) and share when and how Jesus manifested that gift.

Mercy	Healing	Miraculous Powers
Message of Wisdom	_____ (Any Gift) *Jesus Christ*	Prophecy
Evangelism	Leadership	Hospitality

Adapted from Dan Dick and Barbara Dick, *Equipped for Every Good Work* (Wipf & Stock, 2011); equippedforeverygoodwork.wordpress.com. Used by permission.

Spiritual Gifts Bingo

For each of the gifts on this sheet, identify a biblical character you believe possessed that gift. Be sure you can explain why the character fits the gift. In the middle (free) space, choose any gift from those listed in the Spiritual Gifts Descriptions in the *Daily Workbook* (including the three charismatic gifts) and share when and how Jesus manifested that gift.

Pastor-Teacher	Hospitality	Evangelism
Interpretation of Tongues	_____ (Any Gift) *Jesus Christ*	Message of Wisdom
Administration	Leadership	Giving

Adapted from Dan Dick and Barbara Dick, *Equipped for Every Good Work* (Wipf & Stock, 2011); equippedforeverygoodwork.wordpress.com. Used by permission.

Spiritual Gifts Bingo

For each of the gifts on this sheet, identify a biblical character you believe possessed that gift. Be sure you can explain why the character fits the gift. In the middle (free) space, choose any gift from those listed in the Spiritual Gifts Descriptions in the *Daily Workbook* (including the three charismatic gifts) and share when and how Jesus manifested that gift.

Faith	Helps (Serving)	Distinguishing of Spirits
Mercy	_____ (Any Gift) *Jesus Christ*	Message of Knowledge
Teaching	Administration	Miraculous Powers

Adapted from Dan Dick and Barbara Dick, *Equipped for Every Good Work* (Wipf & Stock, 2011); equippedforeverygoodwork.wordpress.com. Used by permission.

A Disciple's Path Evaluation Form

Please help us continue to improve our ministry with new people in our congregation by responding to the following questions. Circle a number from 1 (not at all) to 5 (couldn't be better). Your written comments on ways that we can improve this ministry will be particularly helpful to us as we continue to offer future classes. Thank you!

1. Overall, my first impression of our church.

    1   2   3   4   5

2. People in the congregation have welcomed me and shown a personal interest in me.

    1   2   3   4   5

3. This class has met my expectations in terms of value and quality.

    1   2   3   4   5

4. The class helped me experience Christian community.

    1   2   3   4   5

5. I have learned helpful information and gained valuable insights during this class.

    1   2   3   4   5

6. The class helped me identify how I can serve God in the church and community by helping me understand my spiritual gifts, passion, evangelism style, and ways to live out my faith.

    1   2   3   4   5

7. The class helped me make prayer time and Bible reflection a part of my daily life.

    1   2   3   4   5

8. The homework assignments were helpful and thought provoking.

    1   2   3   4   5

9. The class helped me make a fully informed decision about commitment and membership in this church family.

    1   2   3   4   5

10. Meeting with someone to discuss my gifts helped me to get connected in the church.

    1   2   3   4   5

(continue on back)

If you scored anything less than a 4 on any question, please tell us how we could do better:

Please describe the conversation you had with someone about connecting your gifts with an area of ministry.

The thing I liked most about the class was:

The thing I liked least about the class was:

The new member orientation process could be improved by:

One idea I have for the church or one question I'd like to ask is:

Thanks for your feedback!

(Optional)

Name: _____   Telephone:_____

Email:_____

Wesley Covenant Prayer

I am no longer my own, but thine.

Put me to what thou wilt, rank me with whom thou wilt.

Put me to doing, put me to suffering.

Let me be employed by thee or laid aside for thee,

exalted for thee or brought low by thee.

Let me be full, let me be empty.

Let me have all things, let me have nothing.

I freely and heartily yield all things

to thy pleasure and disposal.

And now, O glorious and blessed God,

Father, Son, and Holy Spirit,

thou art mine and I am thine. So be it.

And the covenant which I have made on earth,

let it be ratified in heaven. Amen.

From *The United Methodist Hymnal* (Nashville: The United Methodist Publishing House, 1989), 607. Used by permission.

Sign-in Sheet

Group Session : _____ **Date:** _____

	Name	E-mail	Phone
1.	_____	_____	_____
2.	_____	_____	_____
3.	_____	_____	_____
4.	_____	_____	_____
5.	_____	_____	_____
6.	_____	_____	_____
7.	_____	_____	_____
8.	_____	_____	_____
9.	_____	_____	_____
10.	_____	_____	_____
11.	_____	_____	_____
12.	_____	_____	_____
13.	_____	_____	_____
14.	_____	_____	_____
15.	_____	_____	_____
16.	_____	_____	_____
17.	_____	_____	_____
18.	_____	_____	_____
19.	_____	_____	_____
20.	_____	_____	_____

Pastor's Coffee Sign-in Sheet

Date: _____

	Name	E-mail	Phone

1. _____
2. _____
3. _____
4. _____
5. _____
6. _____
7. _____
8. _____
9. _____
10. _____
11. _____
12. _____
13. _____
14. _____
15. _____
16. _____
17. _____
18. _____
19. _____
20. _____
21. _____
22. _____
23. _____
24. _____

25. _____
26. _____
27. _____
28. _____
29. _____
30. _____
31. _____
32. _____
33. _____
34. _____
35. _____
36. _____
37. _____
38. _____
39. _____
40. _____
41. _____
42. _____
43. _____
44. _____
45. _____

NOTES

1. Society for Promoting Christian Knowledge, "Classic Prayers," November 1, 2011, http://www.spck.org.uk/classic-prayers/St.-Richard-of-Chichester.
2. Dictionary.com Unabridged. "Disciple," October 4, 2011, http://dictionary.reference.com /browse/disciple.
3. Rueben Job, *A Wesleyan Spiritual Reader* (Nashville: Abingdon Press, 1998), 15.
4. Desmond Tutu, *No Future Without Forgiveness* (New York: Doubleday, 1999), 31.
5. *The United Methodist Handbook* is a 48-page booklet that gives an overview of The United Methodist Church, including a helpful section called "How We Serve," with general information on connectional giving. It is available from www.umcgiving.org or by calling 888-346-3862.
6. Umair Haque, "A Roadmap to Life that Matters," *Harvard Business Review*, July 13, 2011; August 26, 2011, http://blogs.hbr.org/haque/2011/07/a_roadmap_to_a_life_that.html,
7. *The Book of Discipline 2008* (Nashville: The United Methodist Publishing House), ¶125. Used by permission.
8. Dan R. Dick, "Sins of Nomission," United Methodeviations," January 3, 2010, http://doroteos2.wordpress.com/2010/01/13/sins-of-nomission/#more-2659.
9. Frederich Buechner, *Wishful Thinking: A Seeker's ABC*, revised edition (HarperSanFrancisco, 1993), 119.
10. John Ortberg, *The Life You've Always Wanted* (Grand Rapids: Zondervan, 1997), 45-46.